Truth and Toleration in Objectivism

The Contested Legacy of Ayn Rand

Truth and Toleration in Objectivism

The Contested Legacy of Ayn Rand

David Kelley, Ph. D.

The Atlas Society Press

First Edition, 1990
Second Edition, 2000
Third Edition, 2019

Library of Congress Cataloging-in-Publication Data
Kelley, David, 1949–
Truth and Toleration in Objectivism: The Contested Legacy of Ayn Rand / David Kelley — Third Edition
Includes bibliographic references (p. 123–136) and index.
ISBN 978-1-7326037-4-5
1. Rand, Ayn. 2. Objectivism (Philosophy)

Printed in the United States of America
The Atlas Society
800 Rockmead Drive, Suite 200
Kingwood TX 77339

Contents

Preface to the 3rd Edition

2019

Ayn Rand's philosophical novels *The Fountainhead* and *Atlas Shrugged* made her one of the most controversial authors of her age. Her works have drawn millions of readers and continue to sell at a breathtaking pace, and their impact on American culture has been massive. Rand also launched a movement of intellectuals committed to her philosophy of Objectivism. This movement has dramatically expanded the body of literature that articulates her philosophical ideas and develops and applies them to new areas. In the 1960s, Nathaniel Branden founded an institute to promulgate Objectivism through lectures and other means. With Rand herself, he also founded a journal in which most of Rand's philosophical work was first published. In the 50 years since then, the volume of literature has grown by orders of magnitude.

But the Objectivist movement has also seen numerous schisms among its members. Rand's collaboration with Branden came to an end in 1968 with a personal break, one that deeply divided the intellectuals who had gathered around them. *Truth and Toleration* is a short book I wrote in 1990 in the context of another schism, which led to my break with Ayn Rand Institute and the founding of The Atlas Society. A second edition was published in 2000 under the title *The Contested Legacy of Ayn Rand*. In this third edition, we have added a new Postscript and made it available in digital as well as print format.

After 30 years, one might ask, can the events of that time be of more than historical interest? Not in themselves—hardly even to me at this point. But the controversy and the schism were over a philosophical rather than a personal issue, and philosophical issues are not dated. The schism separated two philosophical approaches to Objectivism that have remained separate and antagonistic to this day—especially on the question whether Objectivism is an open or a closed philosophy, as discussed in Chapter 5. Most of this book is concerned with those philosophical issues. By way of background, though, I do want to provide a brief narrative of the events.

After Rand's death in 1982, a second generation of followers launched a number of enterprises to promote her ideas. In 1983, the

Jefferson School began its biannual summer conferences, offering more lectures and courses than any previous event; by 1988, Objectivist summer conferences were an annual affair. In 1985, the Ayn Rand Institute was created to promote Objectivism among students, through essay contests and campus clubs. Lecture courses on Rand's ideas were available on tape, along with publications and a mail-order service for works of interest to Objectivists. The movement was clearly on an upswing, raising hopes that its growth would accelerate and that its ideas would have a wider impact on the cultural and political direction of our society. And accompanying this new optimism—or so it seemed to many of us at the time—was a new spirit of openness and benevolence, our own form of *glasnost.*

The trend was reversed late in the decade, however, largely in reaction to Barbara Branden's 1986 book *The Passion of Ayn Rand,* which the leaders of the movement refused to come to terms with. *Passion* included a candid portrayal of the pressures in Rand's inner circle. It also revealed certain flaws in Rand's own character, intermixed with her many virtues and her prodigious intellect. When the book was published, most of the leaders of the movement followed the example of Leonard Peikoff—Rand's closest associate in her final years and the most prominent exponent of her philosophy—in refusing to discuss it. With their wagons circled in hurt defiance of "the outside world," the movement took on a darker and darker mood, with increasing intolerance toward any criticism of Rand.

At the same time, the libertarian political movement had grown and matured a great deal from its beginnings in the early 1970s. The movement took its inspiration from Rand's passionate defense of capitalism as a moral ideal, as well as from the theories of Austrian economist Ludwig von Mises. Rand vehemently denounced the anarchist strain in libertarianism. She also attacked the strain of expressive individualism that made some libertarians look for common ground with the counterculture and New Left of the period. And she opposed the movement as a whole for its tactic of pursuing political aims without a unified philosophical basis for valuing freedom.

By 1990, however, the movement's center of gravity had shifted from electoral politics to ideas. A growing number of scholars, writers, and policy analysts were laying the intellectual foundations for political change. *Reason* magazine was well on its way to joining the top rank of opinion magazines. The Cato Institute had moved to Washington, D.C., and was establishing a reputation as a major public-policy think tank. The Institute for Humane Studies was rapidly expanding its programs to support classical-liberal students and scholars. The volume of libertarian writing in economics, politics, law, and history had long since passed anyone's ability to read it all.

Many libertarians, moreover, had come to recognize that philosophical and specifically *moral* ideas had to be part of the intellectual foundation. It was particularly clear after the disappointing results of the "Reagan revolution" that the battle for freedom was not going to be won by economic arguments alone. For the large number of libertarian activists whose roots were in Objectivism, who first enrolled in the cause when they read *Atlas Shrugged*—and surveys regularly showed that more libertarians entered the movement through this intellectual route than through any other—this meant a renewed appreciation for Ayn Rand's core ideas: reason, individualism, the value of life in this world. But the Objectivist movement had not shed its antipathy toward libertarians. If anything, the antipathy had become more vehement and extreme, as reflected by Peter Schwartz's essay "Libertarianism: The Perversion of Liberty" (which I discuss in Chapter 2 of this work). And the antipathy was quite mutual on the part of libertarians who derided Objectivism as a dogmatic sect.

This was the social and intellectual context in which I wrote *Truth and Toleration.* I was working as an independent, free-lance writer and speaker. I had published scholarly papers, along with *The Evidence of the Senses,* a work in epistemology, that developed Objectivist philosophical ideas. I was active in the Objectivist movement as a writer and speaker. I was a member of the Ayn Rand Institute's speakers bureau giving talks at its campus clubs around the country and at summer conferences. I had also written a good deal of political commentary that drew attention among libertarians. My interest in opening a dialogue with libertarians, and my refusal to denounce *The Passion of Ayn Rand,* led to a conflict with other leaders of the movement. The conflict deepened when I went beyond these particular casus belli to issue a call for more openness to debate within the movement and for more tolerance toward those outside. As I saw it, these were two sides of the same commitment to reason, objectivity, and respect for the independence of others as individuals. Leonard Peikoff and Peter Schwartz (editor and publisher of *The Intellectual Activist*) wrote articles denouncing me, and the other organs of the movement set in motion the machinery of excommunication. The particulars of these events are described in the original Introduction. The monograph as a whole was my attempt to answer the arguments of Schwartz and Peikoff, to provide the full philosophical case for my own position, and to assess the significance of the issues for the Objectivist movement.

In previous schisms and excommunications, those who were excommunicated went their own way, leaving their more orthodox foes as the only spokesmen for the philosophy. The movement soldiered on, its ranks thinned but unchallenged. But this break was different. With a small group of associates, I founded what is now The Atlas Society. The project drew support from the many Objectivists who had drifted away from the movement over the years, impatient with the true believers in its ranks. At our first public lecture, co-founder George Walsh described the organization as "a home for homeless Objectivists." It was the debut of Objectivism in a new key of openness to debate and of tolerant engagement with other intellectuals and activists, and the launch of a new independent branch of the Objectivist movement.

Neither Peikoff nor Schwartz has replied in print to the critique of their views that you will find in these pages. Indeed, so far as I have been able to determine, none of the people who might be considered principals in the orthodox Objectivist movement—its prominent writers, thinkers, and leaders—has made any effort to address the issues I raised or to answer my arguments. Nevertheless, there has been a great deal of informal debate between critics and defenders of this work, in private conversation, on Internet discussion lists, and in those (relatively few) Objectivist group meetings where the two sides are willing to speak with each other. And for scholars who are interested in Ayn Rand and her impact on American culture, the work provides a useful introduction to the core ideas and central fissures of the Objectivist movement.

We have chosen to republish the text essentially in its original form (with minor copyediting changes) because it played an important historical role as a manifesto in creating a new Objectivist movement; and because I have seen no reason to doubt the essential conclusions regarding moral judgment and sanction, error and evil, causation in the history of ideas, tolerance as a virtue, and Objectivism as an open system. Some of the particulars are now somewhat dated—such as references to the Soviet Union—but readers can easily substitute more timely examples. In addition to the new Postscript, we have included a short article explaining what "open Objectivism" means (Appendix B).

I would like to renew my thanks to the many people who have discussed *Truth and Toleration* with me over the years. My deepest gratitude, however, is to those who have taken the ideas of this work seriously and have had the courage and integrity to act on those ideas: to the staff, trustees, and members of The Atlas Society, past and present; and to all who have joined with us to create a new and healthier Objectivist movement.

Introduction

1990

For as long as there has been an Objectivist movement, its ranks have periodically been thinned by schisms and excommunications, power struggles and purges. I have recently had the opportunity to observe one of these episodes from the inside.

About a year ago, a short essay of mine called "A Question of Sanction" circulated among Objectivists and others. It was a response to an article by Peter Schwartz in *The Intellectual Activist,* demanding that those who speak to libertarians be ostracized from the movement; without mentioning my name, Schwartz made it clear that I was one of his targets.[1] In response, I argued that those who promote ideas we think are false do not automatically deserve moral censure. There's a difference between error and evil. I also observed that Objectivism is not a closed system of belief and that we might actually learn something by talking to people we disagree with. On both counts, I said, we should practice tolerance as a virtue.

Leonard Peikoff then published an article, "Fact and Value," in which he took issue with most of the points I had made.[2] He charged that I repudiated fundamental principles of Objectivism, including the objectivity of values and the necessity of moral judgment. In most cases, he claimed, false ideas are evil, and so are the people who hold them. He added that Objectivism *is* a closed system, and that the movement should be closed along with it. In effect, he invited those who agree with me to leave town.

Unlike most previous purges and schisms in the Objectivist movement, this controversy is essentially philosophical. It's a parting of company over ideas, a conflict between two systematically different views about what Objectivism is and what it means. The controversy was set off by various specific issues regarding moral sanction, but it has brought to the surface, in the form of an explicit difference of opinion, certain pervasive and long-standing differences in the way people understand and practice the philosophy. In "A Question of Sanction," I stated my position in a brief and highly condensed fashion that left many questions unanswered. Since that essay has received a good deal of attention and caused a good deal of turmoil, I feel that a more thorough and systematic treatment of the issues is in order.

Peikoff has said that the essential issue in this debate is the nature of objectivity. I agree. One of Ayn Rand's great insights, the one that gives Objectivism its name, is her recognition that knowledge and values are objective, not intrinsic or subjective. The common thread that runs through every issue in this debate is the question of how to interpret and apply her insight.

As a theory of knowledge, intrinsicism holds that facts are revealed to us, that the mind is a passive mirror, absorbing the truth by revelation or the unthinking acceptance of authority. No effort or activity of thought is required, beyond the effort to open one's mental eyes. So any failure to grasp the truth is a moral failure, a willful refusal to see, properly to be condemned. Subjectivists, on the other hand, argue that knowledge involves a knower who has a specific nature that limits and governs the way he thinks. To reach any conclusion, they say, we have to classify and interpret our experience, and people do this differently, governed by their biases and preconceptions. Subjectivists conclude that we cannot grasp the world as it really is. There is no true and false, only the clash of opinion.

In ethics, the intrinsicist holds that what is right and wrong is determined by certain facts or authorities, and must be accepted as duty, regardless of our own needs and interests as valuers. The subjectivist, on the other hand, denies that right and wrong are revealed to us in this way. He sees *no* objective basis for values. Judgments about right or wrong, good or bad, are merely expressions of our own subjective preferences.

Intrinsicism is characteristic of religious and authoritarian movements; subjectivism has been the hallmark of secular, relativist thought. The clash between them is best captured by Dostoyevsky's statement "If God is dead, everything is permitted." In other words, without a source of revealed truth and intrinsic duties, there can be no objective constraints on belief or action. Ayn Rand rejected this assumption, and saw the clash as a false dichotomy. She faulted intrinsicism for ignoring the fact that knowledge requires a knower, values a valuer. She faulted subjectivism for ignoring the fact that the world exists and is what it is. In epistemology, she said that truth is the grasp of reality by a knower with a specific nature, who employs the method required by his nature: observation, concepts, logic.[3] In ethics, she said that the good is *"an aspect of reality in relation to man."*[4] The good is that which objectively furthers our needs as living beings.

Philosophically, this concept of objectivity is not a compromise or middle way between intrinsicism and subjectivism; it represents a fundamental difference in principle. Fundamentally, the choice is objectivity versus non-objectivity in its various forms. Being objective in practice, however, does require a kind of mental balancing that sometimes feels like striking a compromise. We have to hold in mind the requirements both of reality and of our own nature, and if we focus too narrowly on one or the other, we tend to slide into intrinsicism or subjectivism.

When we insist that facts are facts, that right is right, as against the rampant subjectivism of the age, we can easily forget that facts and values must be grasped by people, each acting on his independent judgment. We run the risk of adopting the attitudes and policies of the intrinsicist. When we emphasize that the true and the good are contextual, when we oppose the imposition of dogma and duty, we can easily forget that opinions and preferences are not all on a par—that some are right and others aren't. We run the risk of subjectivism. To be objective, we have to hold both sets of considerations in mind, both reality and personal context. But that's a delicate balance to maintain in the heat of argument, in the passionate complexity of our engagement with the world and with each other. So it's not surprising that Objectivists should disagree about how to strike the balance, and accuse each other of having sinned in one direction or the other. Within the bounds of reason, this tension is normal and healthy. The jostle of argument and reproach helps all of us keep our balance.

But the current debate has passed the bounds of reason. I have been declared an enemy of Objectivism, and my writings, like those of others before me, have disappeared down the memory hole of the official movement. At Peikoff's insistence, the Ayn Rand Institute has ended its association with me, and is warning the college groups with which it works not to invite me as a speaker. Agreement with his article has been made a loyalty test for participating in Objectivist conferences or working with ARI. This is the behavior of religious zealots. On all theoretical issues that have come up in this debate, moreover, I think it can be proven that my approach is the one required by objectivity, and that

Peikoff's view amounts to intrinsicism. The proof is supplied in the pages that follow.

The first issue concerns the basic relationship between fact and value and its implications for moral judgment. Ayn Rand held that values are rooted in the fact that living things must act to maintain their own survival. Since I agree with her position, I do not accept any dichotomy between fact and value, or between cognition and evaluation. On the contrary, I hold that values are a species of facts, evaluation a species of cognition. But this does not mean that we are obliged to pass moral judgment on every person or action we encounter, as Peikoff claims.

A moral judgment, to be objective, must rest on a large body of evidence, and it normally takes a substantial investment of time and energy to gather the necessary evidence. Peikoff's view that facts wear their value significance on their face, that the moral status of an action or person is revealed in a way that allows us to judge every fact, is a form of epistemological intrinsicism. And his view that we have a duty to judge, without regard to the purpose of judgment, without asking whether it is worth our time and effort to gather the evidence, is a form of moral intrinsicism. In support of these conclusions, I will discuss the nature of the evidence required for judgment (Section I), as well as the implications for action, specifically the nature and proper standards of moral sanction (Section II).

The most important single issue in this debate concerns the distinction I drew between error and evil. In "A Question of Sanction," I observed that "Truth or falsity is the essential property of an idea," a property it has inherently in virtue of its content. An idea can be evaluated good or evil only in relation to some action: either its consequence, the action it leads someone to take; or its cause, the mental action that produced the idea. In regard to the consequences, I will argue in Section III that Peikoff seems to espouse a Hegelian view that ideas enact themselves, that individuals are passive conduits for intellectual forces. In regard to the mental actions that produce ideas, I will show that a philosophical conclusion rests on an enormously complex process of thought in which honest errors are possible at many points. In holding that most positions at variance with Objectivism are inherently dishonest, Peikoff is, once again, giving voice to intrinsicism—a belief that the truth is revealed and that error reflects a willful refusal to see. In light of the objectivity of knowledge and the distinction between error and evil, I will show in Section IV that tolerance is the proper attitude toward people we disagree with, unless and until we have evidence of their irrationality.

The nature of objectivity is the common philosophical thread that runs through all the other issues in this debate: fact and value, moral judgment, and the others. But objectivity is a much broader principle, which bears on a great many other issues as well. Why have these particular issues come to the fore? The answer, I believe, is that all of them have a special bearing on the nature of Objectivism as a philosophy, and its embodiment as a movement. In philosophical terms, this is a debate about what it means to be objective. In psychological terms, however, it's a debate about what it means to be an Objectivist—in a world where most people aren't.

I will address this issue in Section V. As a philosophy of reason, Objectivism must be an open system of thought, where inquiry and debate may take place within the framework of the essential principles that define the system. Peikoff's intrinsicism, by contrast, is reflected in his view of the philosophy as a closed system, defined by certain authorized texts. I will also comment on the kind of movement proper to a philosophy of reason, and on the ways in which the Objectivist movement has fallen short of this standard. The movement has been characterized by a kind of tribalism that we must put behind us if we are to make any progress.

My primary purpose in writing this essay was to elaborate the position I took in "A Question of Sanction." In the course of my work, I found that I had to extend the principles of Objectivism to new areas, and address various questions that have never been raised before. In this respect, the essay is a contribution to Objectivist thought. I would not have written at such length for a purely polemical end. As the foregoing summary indicates, however, I have also undertaken to refute the major claims of my opponents. My remarks will be intelligible to those who have not read the essays by Schwartz and Peikoff, but it should go without saying that those who have not done so will not be in a position to judge the accuracy and fairness of my critique.

I. Moral Judgment

Like every other form of rational action, moral judgment serves a purpose. It is something we must do to pursue our interests, our happiness, our lives. As beings who act with free will, we must judge our own actions in order to steer a proper course and to satisfy our need for self-esteem. And we must judge other people in order to protect ourselves. We want to obtain the benefits of dealing with people who are rational, productive, and fair. We want to avoid being hurt by people who are malicious, cheated by people who are dishonest, exploited by people who are unproductive, or disappointed by those who lack integrity. We also have a stake in the larger political and cultural forces that affect our social environment. We want to foster those that are consistent—and hinder those that are inconsistent—with reason and freedom. To achieve these goals, we must be prepared to pass moral judgment. We must reject not only the traditional religious injunction, "Judge not, that ye be not judged," but also the modern relativist injunction, "Judge not, that ye not hurt someone's feelings." The present controversy, however, has raised a number of questions about the nature of moral judgment, the appropriate standards to employ, and the kind of evidence we need to back up our judgments.

Cognition and Evaluation

Let us begin by putting moral judgment in its wider context. In order to live, man must pursue values. He must therefore *evaluate* things and events in the world, discovering which are good for him and which are bad. Whether something is good or bad, a value or a disvalue, is a fact about its relation to man's life. Values are thus a species of fact. Evaluation, in turn, is a species of cognition: it is our means of grasping the particular type of fact that values represent. We evaluate something by identifying its relationship to a purpose, which provides us with a standard of evaluation. Since life is our fundamental purpose, it is the all-encompassing standard. Fundamentally, there is a single question we ask about anything, whether a thunderstorm, a pesticide, industrial growth, the writing of novels, the telling of lies, the election of candidate X, or whatever. The question is: does it serve our lives or not? If it does, we should encourage and pursue it; if not, we should avoid, change, or eliminate it.

As Ayn Rand demonstrated, values are objective because they rest upon and follow from certain facts about living organisms: that they face an alternative of life or death; that their survival depends on a process of self-generated and self-sustaining action; that they have specific needs and capacities.[1] What she established is that for a living organism, including man, certain facts necessarily have value significance. This is a conclusion of tremendous philosophical importance because it solves the classical "is-ought" problem in ethics; it refutes the claim of moral subjectivists that there is no factual, objective basis for values. It is another question, however, and a much less important one, whether *every* fact has value significance.

Peikoff claims that "every fact bears on the choice to live." The claim is obviously false as stated. The number of hairs in Plato's beard, or blades of grass in Peikoff's lawn, has no bearing on my choice to live. Perhaps in light of such examples, he qualifies the claim by restricting it to the facts *we know about.* His central point is that "cognition implies evaluation," i.e., that "every fact of reality *which we discover* has, directly or indirectly, an implication for man's self-preservation." His argument is that cognition is not an end in itself. Even in the highest reaches of philosophy or mathematics, the function of thought is to serve man's life, not to engage in a disembodied contemplation of the world. The goal of thought, therefore, must be the discovery of those facts that do have "an implication for man's self-preservation."[2]

Even so, Peikoff's claim overstates the case unless it is taken in a highly attenuated sense. From the flood of information pouring through perception, from the mass of information we encounter in reading, conversation, or experience, we become aware of a great many facts. Many of them are irrelevant to our purposes, and we properly disregard them. Others are of such marginal or dubious relevance that it isn't worth our while to ascertain their value significance. For example, one hears of a person who sounds vaguely interesting. Perhaps he would turn out to be a valued friend. But it takes time to get to know someone, and life is short; we simply can't pursue every such lead. The bearing that a given fact may have for our lives is not self-evident; to establish its significance, we must undertake a further process of investigation, including the discovery and integration of other related facts. Any such process takes time and effort, quantities in limited supply. The choice to think about one thing is necessarily a choice *not* to think about others. Evaluation is one of many cognitive functions we must perform, and the resources we devote to it are resources not devoted to others.

In any particular case, therefore, we must decide whether it is worth our while, in light of our purposes, to evaluate a given fact. When we make such a decision, of course, we are passing an *epistemological* value judgment. We are assessing the cognitive worth of a given fact as a datum to be retained, attended to, explored further. In this attenuated sense, it is true without exception that all cognition involves evaluation; the point follows from the fact that cognition is goal-directed. But this is the only conclusion Peikoff's argument will support.

At any rate, the question of whether every fact has value significance, the question to which Peikoff attaches so much importance, is really beside the point. His major accusation against me is that I "sunder fact and value" and thus embrace subjectivism. This is an egregious misrepresentation, based on a logical fallacy. I hold, with Ayn Rand, that every value has a factual basis. This implies that *some* facts have value significance, not that every fact does; the latter is a separate issue.[3] To put it differently, a subjectivist holds that *no* fact has (objective) value significance, and that we are accordingly free to adopt values on the basis of subjective preference or convention. In opposition to this view, objectivity requires that we be prepared to identify the factual basis of all our values, not that we engage in a fevered search for the possible value implications of every fact we encounter.

It should be noted, finally, that none of these issues was raised, even by implication, in "A Question of Sanction." I was concerned there with the specific question of judging other people whose ideas differ from ours. Even if every fact did have value significance, we would still need to ask what the particular value significance of a false belief is; it would not follow automatically that someone who embraces a falsehood is to be judged as evil.[4] I will discuss the issue of error and evil in some detail later. But first let us consider the general nature and grounds of moral judgment.

Moral Judgement

Moral judgment is the particular form of evaluation concerned with what is volitional, with the realm of man-made facts. The distinctive feature of moral judgment is the attribution of moral responsibility, of blame or credit for an action, and this is appropriate only where choice is involved.[5] We praise an act of courage, but not the existence of oxygen; both are good for man, but only the first is a product of choice. For the same reason, we blame a murderer but not a man-eating shark; the consequences are the same for the victim, but the shark is not a volitional agent. Similarly, in judging ourselves, we take pride in our work but not in our shoe size; we feel guilty about a lie, but not about being near-sighted.

Since the fundamental choice is whether to think or not, whether to use our capacity for reason, we must judge people by how they make this choice.[6] In judging an action, therefore, we are concerned not only with its consequences, measured by the standard of life, but also with its source in the person's motives, as measured by the standard of rationality. The question is how to integrate these two factors into a single judgment. Philosophers have long wrestled with this question; they have proposed various theories about the proper weight to assign to consequences on the one hand and motives on the other. The Objectivist ethics, unfortunately, has yet to address this question in any depth. But it's clear that we cannot ignore either factor.

If we consider only the consequences, we may still evaluate an action in the same way we evaluate a natural occurrence like a hurricane. To pass a *moral* judgment, however, we must consider the motives that inspired the action. There's obviously a moral difference between a person who kills someone accidentally, while playing with a loaded gun, and a cold-blooded killer who shoots his victim deliberately. The consequences are the same, but not the moral status of the agents. The first may be blamed for negligence, for evading the risks of a loaded weapon, and to that extent he is responsible for what happened. But he does not bear the same degree of guilt, morally or legally, as the murderer who consciously intended to bring about the consequence, and who had to evade on a much larger scale in order to have such an intention. When we judge an action morally, in other words, we cannot consider the effects in isolation from the person's volitional control over them.

Nor should we make the opposite error of judging the inner element of choice in isolation from the action it produces. A long line of thinkers, of whom Immanuel Kant is the clearest instance, argued that if we can judge an action only in virtue of its volitional character, then the act of volition itself is the real object of judgment; we may *evaluate* the action and its effects, but *morally* speaking it is only the motive that counts. This is fallacious. It is like the epistemological fallacy of assuming that if we perceive an object only in virtue of the way it appears to us, then strictly speaking it is only the appearance, not the object itself, that we perceive.[7] In fact, what we perceive is the object-as-it-appears, and what we judge is the action-as-it-was-chosen. If we divorce the inner choice from the outer action, then we divorce the standard of rationality from the standard of life. But rationality is a means to an end, not an end in itself. If reason did not help us pursue and maintain our lives—if it made no difference whether we thought well, or poorly, or not at all—then rationality would not be a virtue nor a standard of judgment. In moral judgment, as in any other type of evaluation, life is the fundamental and all-encompassing standard.

There is an obvious moral difference between the person who evades his goal of losing weight, and indulges a desire for a second helping of dessert, and a totalitarian dictator who evades the sanctity of human life and murders millions of his subjects. Both people evaded; they both did something wrong, worthy of blame. But there is an enormous difference in degree. The dieter's mental action was a minor lapse, easily repaired; the dictator's was immense and irreparable. We measure the degree of irrationality by considering the scope and value significance of the foreseeable consequences that were evaded. If we consider the mental act of choice in isolation, we will tend to view evasion as intrinsically wrong, apart from its consequences, and will thus view all acts of evasion as morally equivalent.[8] (I believe this is one source of the phenomenon I described in "A Question of Sanction": the tendency of some Objectivists to ignore differences in degree of wrongdoing, and thus to engage in moral hysteria, the ringing condemnation of the venial.)

In light of these general principles, let us now consider the actual process of forming and validating a moral judgment.

Types of Moral Judgement

It would take a separate treatise to lay out the different types of moral judgment and the evidence appropriate to each. But I want to discuss a few of the relevant issues in order to indicate the kind of thinking that objectivity requires in this area. For purposes of analysis, we may distinguish four different kinds of conclusions, in order of the amount of evidence we need to justify them: evaluating an action, interpreting its motive, inferring a character trait, and judging that someone is good or bad as a person.

1) Evaluating actions. Before we can judge an action morally, we must evaluate it in the wider sense I described above. We must ask whether the action was good or bad, using life as our fundamental standard. The requirements of human life are so various, however, and the effects of a given action so complex, that we cannot apply the standard directly to concretes. We need principles that identify the *kinds* of things that are good and bad, and the kinds of actions that will promote the one or the other. To evaluate a particular action, therefore, we must identify its nature conceptually, and then apply to it the appropriate moral principles. Our procedure is basically deductive: action X is a case of type Y (telling a lie, being productive, breaking a contract, etc.); Y is good (or bad); therefore, X is good (or bad). But there are certain inductive factors to consider as well, and we are guilty of rationalism if we ignore them.

One is the matter of degree. I pointed out in "A Question of Sanction" that "When we formulate moral principles, we abstract from differences of degree; we omit measurements, as Ayn Rand explained. But when we *apply* the principles in forming moral judgments about particulars, we must reintroduce the relevant measurements." It is wrong to take someone's property without his consent. This principle omits the measurements of what is taken: its value to the owner, its replaceability, etc. But we must specify these measurements to know the *degree* of wrong done by a thief. It is worse to embezzle a person's life savings than to steal an apple from his tree.[9]

The kind of measurement involved here, as Ayn Rand observed, is ordinal rather than cardinal.[10] There is no unit that would allow us to measure an action in cardinal terms—to say, for example, that it promoted the actor's life by a factor of 2.36. We are limited to ordinal measurement, which is essentially comparative: action A was better than action B, but not as good as action C. When we evaluate an action, therefore, we must compare it to other actions of the same type, noting the similarities and differences relevant to the moral issue involved, so that we can assign the action its place on the scale of good and bad. This approach is essentially inductive, because it means sifting through our experience to find comparable actions. It is the only way to avoid the twin errors of moral sentimentality (exaggerating the degree of good) and moral hysteria (exaggerating the degree of evil).

Another inductive factor arises when the effects of an action and the circumstances in which it occurred are complex, so that different principles apply in virtue of different features of the action. A teenager lies to his parents about whether he is still seeing a girlfriend of whom they disapprove. If we consider his action merely as a lie, we would conclude that it is wrong. But this may not be the only relevant feature. If the parents' disapproval is irrational—if it is based on a puritanical view of sex, for example, or racial or ethnic prejudice against the girl—then the boy may also be seen as acting to protect a value against injustice.

When we judge an action, we must try to identify all the relevant facts, and the corresponding principles, some of which may not be obvious at first glance. In cases of any complexity, such as actions that occur in the context of a personal or business relationship, this normally means that we must give a hearing to all the parties involved, therefore allowing everyone to tell his side of the story. And secondly we must integrate the facts and principles, giving each one due weight in our conclusion. We may decide that one aspect of the situation is essential, and should govern our assessment (the nature of the parents' irrationality may be such that the boy had no obligation to tell the truth). Or we may decide that one factor mitigates another (the lie was wrong but pardonable in the circumstances). But we cannot simply ignore any relevant fact.

2) Interpreting motives. To judge an action morally, we must consider motive as well as consequence. We must ask what goal the person was trying to pursue, and what connection he saw between his action and his goal, so that we can assess his rationality in choosing to act as he did. It is rare that we can read the motive directly from the act, as Peikoff suggests we can when he contrasts the architect with the murderer. To have built a skyscraper, the architect "must have expended mental effort, focus, work," and in that respect is certainly entitled to a positive moral judgment.[11] But it would make a difference to our judgment whether this mental effort sprang from a love of production, or from a desire to make more money than his college classmate, or from a desire to escape the chaos of his personal life. Peter Keating built skyscrapers, too.

Some evidence about a person's motives may be acquired directly, by observing the manner in which he acts—his facial expression, tone of voice, "body language," and other emotional clues to which human beings, from infancy on, are highly sensitive. But this sort of evidence is limited to cases we observe first-hand. The perception of emotions is governed by a great many factors, many of which cannot be put into words, so it is generally not valid to put much weight on someone else's impressions. And this sort of evidence is limited to the *emotions* a person is expressing. We do not have the same sensitivity to the long-range goals or the thought processes that produced the action.

Normally, therefore, the interpretation of a motive has the logical status of a hypothesis we introduce to explain an action, and we must follow the same rules of evidence that scientists use to validate their hypotheses. We cannot justify the attribution of a motive solely on the grounds that it *would* explain the behavior we observe. Some other motive might also explain the behavior. We must show that a given motive provides the *only* or the *best* explanation. This requires that we consider other possible motives, and ask which is most consistent with everything we know about the person's character and past behavior. We must be careful not to leap at the first motive that occurs to us, with the attitude "What other explanation could there be?" Invariably, there is one. Nor can we assume, when an action appears to have violated a moral principle, that the person must have evaded that principle. He may not have been in a position to grasp its bearing on the situation. Or he may have considered the principle and decided it did not apply, or was outweighed in light of other facts. The best way to avoid these hasty judgments is normally to ask the person. His explanation will not always be a reliable guide, especially if his motives were not honorable, or not conscious. But we cannot safely ignore it.

3) Inferring character traits. A motive consists of the values and beliefs on which a person acts in a particular case. A character trait is defined by certain values and beliefs on which a person *characteristically* acts. Thus the relation of a motive to a character trait is that of a concrete instance to a general rule. Judgments about character are perhaps the most common and most important of our moral judgments. To decide whether and how we want to deal with someone, we need to predict how he will act in the future: Is he reliable? Will he tell the truth? Will he carry his weight? Will he act with integrity and courage when the going gets rough? Such predictions depend on an assessment of the person's character. But our knowledge of his character is a generalization from the way he has acted in the past, and the motives with which he acted. So the question is: when is it valid to generalize? What evidence is relevant to inferring a character trait from the motives at work in particular actions?

If humans were like inanimate objects, there would be no great problem. When we observe a lump of sugar dissolving in water, we may infer at once that sugar will always dissolve in similar circumstances: it has the *trait* of water-solubility. But man has free will. It is possible for him to act out of character, to evade his knowledge of the values and principles on which he normally acts. One student cheats on an exam because he thought he could get away with it; he is a chronic amoralist, seeking to pass by any means; he feels regret but not guilt when he is caught. Another cheats because he is floundering in the course and under intense pressure from his family to get good grades; afterwards, when he has time to reflect, he feels ashamed and comes forward voluntarily to confess. Both students did something wrong, and both acted from bad motives: the desire to gain a value by faking reality. In the first case, however, this motive is typical for the person; it flows from his character; he is a dishonest person. In the second case, the motive was atypical; a basically honest person acted out of character.

How can we say that this student was honest, even in a qualified way? Doesn't any violation of a moral principle destroy the principle? It is important here to distinguish philosophy from psychology. Philosophically, moral principles are (contextually) absolute. To admit any exception—to say that it is sometimes okay to fake reality, or replace justice by favoritism, or whatever—is to abandon the principle. But it does not follow, as Peikoff suggests elsewhere, that someone who commits a moral lapse has psychologically abandoned his principles, or that "To be evil 'only sometimes' *is* to be evil."[12] There's a difference between someone who adopts the pragmatist policy of being honest only 99% of the time, and someone who is committed to 100% honesty as a matter of principle but fails on a given occasion. Peikoff's claim is true of the first but not of the second.

When we infer a character trait from a particular action, therefore, we need to know whether the act reflected a standing policy, or whether it was an aberration. So we must ask certain questions: Is the action consistent with the way the person has acted in the past—is there a pattern of such behavior? Was the action taken in circumstances of unusual pressure, or intense emotion, that distorted the person's judgment? And how does the person himself view his action when he's had time to think about it? In regard to this last point, it is customary to ask for an apology. The function of apologies is not to enjoy the spectacle of someone's self-abasement, but to find out whether he endorses or renounces his action.

The discovery that a certain action was an aberration does not mean we must erase it from the person's record, or extend immediate forgiveness. If someone lied under pressure, for example, we're entitled to conclude that he is capable of giving in to such pressure, unless and until we see him do better in the future. It's also true that some actions are so destructive that an immediate judgment about character is justified, on the ground that the evasion involved would have to be so massive that it could not be an isolated occurrence. Cold-blooded murder is an example. But there aren't many others. In the cases most of us encounter in our lives, we need more detailed information about the person's background and circumstances.

4) Judging the person. It is possible for a person to be rational in some respects, or some areas of life, but not in others. It is possible to possess virtues as well as vices. Someone may be honest but not productive. He may be just in dealing with his employees, but not in dealing with his children. How do we judge a person as a whole? When is it appropriate to regard a specific character flaw as grounds for condemning the person as such, as a person? In my view, there are two broad factors to consider.

The first is the person's own attitude toward the trait. Is he aware of it? If so, does he embrace it as part of his identity, or does he distance himself from it, treating it as he would a physical wound or blemish, as something to be fixed or removed? I noted above that if someone apologizes for a particular action and renounces the motive behind it, then we cannot take that motive as evidence of a general vice. The same principle applies one level up. If a person is aware of a vice and is trying to change it, we cannot hold the person to be corrupt *in toto*. On the contrary, we should respect that part of him which is making the effort.

The second factor to consider is the scope and the depth of the flaw in the person's character. Before we condemn the person as such, we must assure ourselves that the flaw is *essential* to his character, underlying and explaining many of his other characteristics. The flaw must be a dominant theme of the person, coloring much of what he does or feels or says. Not every character trait can play such a role. Punctuality is a virtue, for example, and someone who is never on time for anything is irresponsible. But the irresponsibility is delimited. It is not like the fundamental and pervasive irresponsibility of an emotionalist who cannot carry out any long-range plan or sustain a commitment; who never gives thought to the consequences of his action; who lives in chronic dependence on others, without concern for the havoc he wreaks in their lives. The emotionalist deserves our moral censure as a person; the unpunctual man does not.

This kind of censure is the farthest-reaching judgment we can make about another person, and accordingly it requires the most evidence. Except in the case of larger-than-life figures who have acted on the public stage, and whose words and deeds have been recorded by historians, it requires extensive first-hand knowledge of the person. It is not often that we know someone well enough to understand the role in his character of the traits we observe, or the nature of his attitude toward those traits. Fortunately, it is not often that we need to make such judgments. I know nothing about the romantic life of the mechanic who fixes my car, and I don't need to know; it's enough that he gets the job done and stands behind his work. Most of our relationships with others are limited, and we need to be concerned only with the particular traits relevant to a given relationship.

The Temperament of a Judge

The foregoing was a brief outline of the factors that a reasonable person, someone of good judgment, takes into account in judging others. Though the factors are numerous, and somewhat complex, there is nothing arcane about them. They reflect the dictates of common sense within the context of the Objectivist moral code. But they make it clear that judgment requires thought. We must be clear about the nature of the conclusion we are drawing: are we merely evaluating an action from the outside, or passing a moral judgment? In the latter case, are we judging an action, a character trait, or someone's character as a whole? At each level, we must take account of all the relevant facts, giving the person himself a fair hearing, considering alternative explanations of his action, and noticing differences of degree. In short, we must exercise what lawyers call a "judicial temperament": the ideal judge's scrupulous attention to the facts and impartial application of standards. This approach is required by justice. Moral judgment is concerned not with inanimate objects but with people. Given man's need for morality and self-esteem, no one can view the assessment of his actions or character with complete indifference. This is what makes moral judgment so powerful a weapon for defending the good and punishing the evil. It is not a weapon to be shot from the hip.

The judicial temperament does not appear to be what Peikoff has in mind when he describes the approach of the moralist or valuer:

> A valuer, in [Ayn Rand's] sense, is a man who evaluates extensively and intensively. That is: he judges ***every*** fact within his sphere of action—and he does it passionately, because his value-judgments, being objective, are integrated in his mind into a consistent whole, which to him has the feel, the power, and the absolutism of a direct perception of reality.[13]

This description of the valuer calls for comment on several levels.

I have already observed that it is impossible to evaluate extensively in Peikoff's sense—to evaluate literally every fact of which we become aware. The point is of crucial importance when we consider moral judgments about other people. The requirements of objectivity are such that in many cases we lack the evidence we need to form a moral judgment. We must then ask whether it is worth our while to acquire the relevant evidence, and the answer will often be "No." Judging others is not the only or the most important claim on our time and effort.

Of course we should draw any moral conclusions that do follow from the evidence at hand, and we should make the effort to acquire evidence whenever a moral judgment would have an important bearing on our relationship to someone. But we cannot devote our lives to the task of investigating everyone with whom we come in contact, so that we may judge them fairly. And no one does so. But if we accept Peikoff's sweeping injunction to judge, then we are liable to judge people *without* investigating all the facts: to judge unfairly, nonobjectively, on insufficient evidence.

This danger is accentuated by Peikoff's claim about the intensive character of judgments: that they should have "the feel, the power, and the absolutism" of perception. It is intrinsicism to maintain that the moral status of an action or a person is self-evident, like a perceptual judgment. *After* we have reached a conclusion, and integrated it with the rest of our knowledge, it may come to seem self-evident, because we have automatized the relevant integrations. But in the *process* of reaching a conclusion, of arriving at a judgment, we must go through the steps consciously. For all the reasons I have stated, this process requires thought. The application of a moral principle is rarely obvious, and should never be automatic.[14] Given the link Ayn Rand observed between intrinsicism and emotionalism, moreover, Peikoff's reference to passion is significant. He does not distinguish very clearly, here or elsewhere in his essay, between evaluation and emotion. Evaluation is a species of cognition; emotion is not. An emotion *flows from* an evaluation of its object, and does so automatically. But the evaluation itself is a cognitive product, and to be valid it must rest on the cognitive process of weighing the evidence.

There are two levels of intrinsicism, then, in Peikoff's account of the valuer. It is epistemological intrinsicism to compare moral judgment with perception, to treat the moral status of a person as a fact that reveals itself without the need for extensive integration and the exercise of a judicial temperament. It is ethical intrinsicism to treat moral judgment as an out-of-context duty, rather than a function we perform in accordance with our hierarchy of values. But there is an even deeper problem with his account.

In this passage, and throughout the essay, Peikoff's focus is on evaluation, and even more narrowly, on moral judgment. Evaluation and judgment are responses to what exists, sorting the things that pass before us into categories of good, bad, and indifferent. But a rational life, the life of a valuer, does not consist essentially in reaction. It consists in action. Man does not find his values, like the other animals; he creates them. The primary focus of a valuer is not to take the world as it comes and pass judgment. His primary focus is to identify what might and ought to exist, to uncover potentialities that he can exploit, to find ways of reshaping the world in the image of his values. This is the essence of Ayn Rand's exalted view of man as a heroic being of unlimited potential. To be a valuer in her sense is to be a creator, not merely a critic.[15] Evaluation and judgment are certainly necessary to the creation of value, but they are means to an end, not ends in themselves. If we drop this context, we run the risk of turning her wonderful vision into a crabbed and carping moralism. Moral judgment is an important function in a rational life. It is part of one's daily moral hygiene. But it is not what life is about.

II. Sanction

Objectivism holds that evil is impotent in itself, that it can flourish only with the aid of the good, and thus that one has a grave moral responsibility not to provide such aid.[1] This is the insight that drives the plot of *Atlas Shrugged*. But it is rarely obvious how to apply this principle, how to decide what particular actions it requires in the myriad circumstances of actual life. For years, Objectivists have been debating the propriety of actions such as attending the Bolshoi Ballet or buying Polish ham; subscribing to (or writing for) publications with a conservative (or libertarian, or liberal) slant; attending public universities, or teaching at such universities, or working in other government jobs, or accepting government grants; buying works written by people who have been purged from the Objectivist movement, or maintaining personal or professional relationships with them.

In order to reach a conclusion about any particular case, we must first establish whether the individuals or groups involved are evil, and in what respects. That is, we must pass moral judgment, using the method described in the preceding section.[2] We must then determine whether the actions in question constitute impermissible aid. How do we do so? In this section I will discuss the relevant principles to employ. I will then apply those principles to the issue of speaking to libertarian groups, the issue that gave rise to this entire controversy.

Existential Aid and Moral Sanction

The principle that we should not contribute to evil covers two broad categories of action pertaining to existence and consciousness. Because evil consists in irrationality, it is inefficacious in itself. Irrational people and groups can succeed existentially only through the aid of the rational. So we should avoid giving them the benefit of our time, energy, or money, or in any other way contributing causally to their success. Because of the inescapable role of morality in man's life, moreover, evil can succeed only by disguising itself. It must disarm its victims morally by presenting itself as the good. Even petty criminals are quick to excuse their predations with self-justifying rationalizations. Evil on the larger scale represented by a destructive political movement always employs ideology and propaganda to clothe itself in the moral dress of idealism. Evil is threatened by the conscious recognition of its nature. We must therefore withhold from it our sanction, our approval, our moral blessing.

These two issues of existential aid and conscious sanction are intimately related, as are existence and consciousness in general. Evil needs the sanction of the good precisely in order to win the allegiance of those who will then provide it with aid. Irrational causes seek endorsement by public figures, for example, for the purpose of raising funds. Sanction may thus be regarded as a special form of aid. But it *is* special: it has certain features that distinguish it from other contributions to evil.

Let us begin, then, by considering existential aid in general. The first thing to note is that it's impossible to avoid every such contribution. Most of our transactions in the world are with people of mixed character. We should certainly try to make sure that our relationships with them are based on their virtues, their rational elements, not their vices. This policy is our only protection against the direct and obvious dangers of irrationality; it is also the means of obtaining the long-range benefit of rewarding virtue and discouraging vice. But we have no control over how a person will use the benefits he obtains from us. A worker who is highly rational on the job may devote his earnings to an irrational cause, or an after-hours life of debauchery. People are unitary beings. We may choose to deal with them only to the extent that they are rational, but it is rare that we can tailor the exchange so that it benefits only their rational side.

The same is true on a larger social scale. It is a basic truth of economics that in any voluntary trade, both parties benefit. It is also true that in an economic system with a complex division of labor and integrated markets, every transaction has some effect on every other transaction. As long as we act economically, therefore, it is impossible to avoid aiding evil people and groups at least indirectly. In varying degrees, the benefits of our action will fall upon the just and the unjust alike. For example, one may properly refuse to make any direct loan to a totalitarian government. But *any* money one saves will marginally increase the supply of capital, and thus lower the prevailing rate of interest. So, as long as the totalitarian government has access to the international capital market, it will benefit from one's savings.

The same basic point applies, finally, to the marketplace of ideas, as I argued in "A Question of Sanction." One cannot participate in this marketplace without conferring some benefits on ideas one opposes, at least in an indirect and attenuated way. When a writer contributes to a magazine, for example, he has to assume that his article will help the magazine retain and expand its audience; the article would not have been accepted otherwise. And this in turn will benefit all other contributors to the magazine, including those whose ideas the writer opposes. In the same way, publishing a successful book will allow one's publisher to put out other books. Obtaining a Ph.D. in philosophy helps that philosophy department maintain its graduate program, and thus the ability to impress its ideas on future students. *Every* action one might take in the marketplace of ideas will have similar effects.

It is important to understand that the principle of withholding aid from evil is not an ethical primary. It is derived from the fundamental values of life and happiness, which imply an extensive hierarchy of other values. The principle is valid only within this context, which must be kept in mind whenever we consider the danger of aiding evil in a particular case. We cannot let the fear of doing harm keep us from pursuing all positive values; that would be to make evil potent indeed. The positive value of providing for our future and investing in production requires that we save our money. The positive value of spreading our ideas requires that we participate in the marketplace of ideas. These are not values we can abandon merely because the actions have some untoward consequences.

Within this context, our goal should be to avoid aiding evil any more than necessary. We should make sure that any such aid is an unavoidable byproduct of a rational purpose. We should try to tailor our action so as to minimize such aid. And we should avoid the action when the evil is of a magnitude that outweighs the positive benefits of the action. These commonsense standards require that we weigh the costs and benefits of an action, including the particular *degree* of good and bad that may result. This is not a policy of pragmatism, as Schwartz alleges.[3] A benefit is a value, and a cost is a disvalue. The essence of pragmatism is not its concern with costs and benefits; that concern is shared by any value-oriented, teleological ethics, including Objectivism. The essence of pragmatism is its claim that costs and benefits can be measured without the use of principles. That is why, as the old joke says, pragmatism doesn't work.

Moral principles tell us what kinds of things are valuable or harmful, beneficial or costly to our lives. They tell us which traits of people are virtuous and vicious, and thereby tell us whom it is in our interest to deal with. To pursue our interests, therefore, we must act on principle: the moral is the practical. This point is not in dispute. But Schwartz writes as if every action we consider is governed by a single principle. In fact, this is almost never the case. The circumstances in which we act are normally complex, and the consequences various. We use principles to identify the goods and ills at stake, but we must then weigh the good against the ill, in the manner I've indicated. This normally requires that we consider specific degrees of good or harm. For example, we do not hesitate to put our money into savings instruments, despite the fact that we thereby lower the cost of loans to evil governments, because the benefits are substantial and the harm negligible. These are quantitative judgments, and they are not always this obvious. Such weighing of costs and benefits is the only possible method of acting on principle, and it is therefore morally required of us: the practical is the moral.

Let us now turn to the issue of sanction. The term "sanction" has often been used by Objectivists to cover all contributions to evil, including existential aid. This has bred needless confusion. The term refers to the action of endorsing or approving something. To sanction is to express a conscious judgment that something is good, right, honorable, legitimate, etc. Obviously, we should not sanction evil, any more than we should provide it with existential aid. But there's a difference in the nature of our control over these effects. When we act in the world, the consequences depend not only on our intentions but also on the circumstances in which we act. For the reasons given above, the pursuit of any value normally has the side-effect of conferring some benefit—somehow, in some degree— on people or ideas we would not choose to benefit. Since we cannot suspend the law of causality, we cannot avoid this cost; we can only minimize it. But we do have full control over what we sanction. We can discriminate in thought between good and bad, even when they are causally linked in reality, and express our approval of the one alongside our disapproval of the other.

Because sanction is a matter of conscious judgment, it is normally conveyed in words. We sanction a thing by saying so. In this respect, the act of sanctioning is like the act of promising. It is not something we can do inadvertently. If we want to know whether we have sanctioned a certain action, person, or idea, we need only consider our conscious judgment about it, and whether we have expressed that judgment. For the same reason, we find out what someone else sanctions by asking him.

There are cases, however, in which sanction is expressed by actions other than speech. The possibility of such nonverbal sanction is at the root of many controversies among Objectivists, and has bred a good deal of fear about inadvertently sanctioning something one shouldn't. But this phenomenon occurs much less often than many people think. Sanction is not a magical substance, conveyed by contact. We can accuse someone of sanctioning an evil nonverbally only if his action can reasonably be interpreted as expressing a positive moral assessment of it. And the standard of what is reasonable is set by the requirements of pursuing values in the world. In my opinion, for example, the purchase of a good imported from a communist country does not raise an issue of sanction. One may choose not to buy the product because one does not want to contribute financially to such a government. But there is no issue of sanction *per se*, because there is no presumption in a free market economy that the buyer of a good morally approves of its manufacturer.

In regard to the marketplace of ideas, it is important to understand that concern about sanction is not unique to Objectivism. Most people who work with ideas hold views to which they are deeply committed, and they are wary of acting in such a way as to imply any endorsement of opposing ideas. The guiding principle here was identified by Ayn Rand: "In any *collaboration* between two men (or two groups) who hold *different* basic principles, it is the more evil or irrational one who wins."[4] But this principle cannot be interpreted as a ban on intellectual contact among those who disagree. To allow for the discussion of ideas without the sacrifice of anyone's integrity, those who work with ideas have devised a number of arm's-length relationships, for arms of different lengths. These relationships define the types and degrees of endorsement that can reasonably be attributed to the participants.

Co-authoring a book, for example, is a fairly intimate form of collaboration. In the absence of an explicit proviso, it implies an endorsement of everything in the work, even passages written by the other author. Appearing in a debate or public discussion with another person is a much looser form of association. The personal nature of the contact implies some respect for him as a person and thinker, but not necessarily any endorsement of his views, and it would be dubious to describe this as collaboration. An even longer arm's-length relationship is involved in giving an invited speech to a group, where one has the platform to himself, and has no idea what other speakers may be invited in the future. The speaker's appearance does sanction the group in a minimal way: one may properly assume that he regards the group as falling within the realm of civilized discourse. But there is no implication that he endorses the ideas of the group, even if it has a definite ideological commitment. Ideological groups, no less than those of a more ecumenical spirit (like the Ford Hall Forum), may invite speakers representing different points of view in order to consider the arguments against their own position. Providing this service implies no endorsement of that position, and it would be twisting words beyond recognition to describe it as collaboration.[5]

The Case Of Libertarianism

A case in point was the incident that spawned this entire controversy: a speech I gave to the Laissez Faire Supper Club. The sponsors of the Supper Club are libertarians in political philosophy. I went there to explain why the defense of liberty depends on certain fundamental principles that are central to Objectivism—specifically, the principles that reason is an absolute, that one's own happiness is the moral purpose of life, and that there is no dichotomy between mind and body. In the course of my talk, I criticized libertarians who try to defend freedom on the basis of subjectivism (as well as conservatives who try to defend it on the basis of mysticism and altruism). These points were clearly summarized in the description of my talk in the Laissez Faire Books catalog. I am therefore on record as having refused to endorse, approve, or sanction any subjectivist variety of libertarianism. It would be entirely irrational to attribute to me a moral judgment that I not only haven't made, but have explicitly and publicly rejected. Given the content of my talk, it cannot be interpreted as a collaborator with an ideological opponent, subject to the principle of Ayn Rand's I cited above. Instead, it falls under another of her rules for relating princples to goals: "When opposite basic principles are clearly and openly defined, it works to the advantage of the rational side."[6]

Of course I am assuming the Supper Club is comparable to other ideological groups of a liberal, conservative, or socialist bent. I am assuming that its ideology does not represent the kind or degree of irrationality that would put the group outside the realm of civilized intellectual exchange. This is an assumption that Schwartz rejects. In his initial critique of my appearance at the Supper Club, he compared libertarians to communist dictators. In his reply to my "Question of Sanction," he compares them to the totalitarian theocrats of Khomeini's Iran. Therefore, in his view, even the minimal sanction one confers by the mere act of speaking to them is unwarranted—regardless of what one says.

What grounds does Schwartz have for these bizarre analogies? Laissez Faire Books does not run a Gulag Archipelago of concentration camps, nor does it advocate a medieval fundamentalist theocracy. It has not issued a murder contract on an author it doesn't like. Schwartz regards these differences as superficial. In his view, the movement is committed essentially to nihilism: the desire to obliterate reality, reason, and values. Its adherents, he says, are motivated by hatred of the state, not because it violates rights but because it imposes restraints—and they are equally opposed to the restraints imposed by morality and logic. Such nihilism is the deepest form of irrationality, equivalent to that of communist dictators or Islamic fundamentalists, and would have equivalent results in practice. This nihilism is pervasive in the libertarian movement, Schwartz believes, and Laissez Faire Books is a major source of libertarian literature. Therefore one should boycott that organization.[7]

This whole chain of reasoning hangs from the premise that libertarians are nihilists. The evidence Schwartz offers for this generalization is partly inductive. He cites various libertarian theorists who are skeptics in epistemology or subjectivists in ethics, who deny that liberty need be grounded on anything more than the desire for it, who applaud any attack on the state regardless of its motives or effects, and who are consequently drawn to support all manner of unsavory causes, such as the terrorism of Yassir Arafat. This element of the movement is more than a lunatic fringe; in the past, for example, it has been pervasive in the Libertarian Party. But this element does not define the movement as such. The most prominent organizations in the movement, such as the Cato Institute, do not espouse such views and have taken steps to distance themselves from those who do. The intellectual leaders acknowledged by most libertarians and promoted most heavily by Laissez Faire Books include not only Ayn Rand and Murray Rothbard, but also writers such as Milton Friedman, Ludwig von Mises, Friedrich von Hayek, Thomas Sowell, and Robert Nozick. None of them is a nihilist, and none is mentioned in Schwartz's essay. His inductive evidence, in short, consists in a highly selective, non-representative sample.

Schwartz is aware of this fact. He acknowledges that many libertarians do not share the views he ascribes to them. So he offers a deductive argument to prove that those views are nonetheless implicit in the movement as its essence. Libertarianism is a political ideology defined in abstraction from any philosophical basis; the movement accordingly is a coalition of people who share a political viewpoint but may disagree on everything else. The attempt to create such a coalition, he argues, implies the view that liberty does not require any philosophical defense; this view is based on subjectivism, which leads to all the consequences he outlines; therefore libertarians are nihilistic subjectivists, whether they know it or not.

Once again, this chain of deductions is rationalistic. It is one thing to hold that the advocacy of liberty does not require any objective philosophical basis. It is another thing—and in my experience a more common view among libertarians—to hold that liberty does have an objective basis, but that one may make common cause with those who subscribe to a basis other than one's own. Beyond a certain point, which I tried to define in my talk to the Supper Club, this latter view is an error. To see why it is an error, however, one must understand the role of philosophy in social change and the hierarchical relationships among the branches of philosophy; and to understand these matters, one must in turn understand the nature of concepts and of man's need for morality. None of this is self-evident; the derivations are neither simple nor obvious; honest errors are possible at many points. We cannot assume *a priori* that those who fail to embrace our position are nihilists.

And if they indicate an interest in our position, why shouldn't we make an effort to explain it to them?

Schwartz complains that having invited me to speak on Objectivism, libertarians might later invite a religious defender of freedom, then an amoralist, etc. "They lap this up. It is all entirely consistent with Libertarianism. It is consistent with the philosophy that philosophies and reasons are irrelevant to a belief in liberty."[8] Perhaps. But it is also consistent with the belief that philosophy is crucial to the defense of liberty, so that it's crucial to discover which philosophy is correct. The latter is surely the more likely hypothesis about their motives. Why would a group bother to invite philosophers at all if they thought philosophy irrelevant? In effect, Schwartz is berating all libertarians as irrational because they do not accept Objectivism at one swallow. If they wish to learn about Objectivism, he asserts with the breath-taking arrogance of a Bourbon king, let them come to us: "The existence of Objectivism is widely known throughout the Libertarian movement. It is certainly not difficult for any of its members to seek information about it *outside* the confines of libertarianism, where there arc writers and speakers available to enlighten them."[9] Such demands are unwarranted, self-defeating, and frankly stupid.

Underlying this dispute about libertarianism, however, there is a much more general and fundamental difference between my position and Schwartz's. He claims that libertarians are not only mistaken in their views, but evil in character. They are guilty of a moral error, not merely an error of knowledge. This judgment about an entire class of people is obviously not based on knowledge of them as individuals, nor on the kind of process I described in the preceding section. The general question is whether this sort of inference is valid. Does ideology provide a shortcut to moral judgment? Does intellectual error imply immorality? This is the issue which I raised in "A Question of Sanction," and to which Peikoff's essay is largely devoted. It is time to address the issue in its general form.

III. Error and Evil

Objectivist thought is not an ivory tower doctrine, an exercise in pure contemplative thought. It is a fighting creed. It holds that ideas—philosophical ideas above all—shape the lives of individuals and the fate of nations. When we observe the disastrous consequences of the ideas of Kant or Hegel, and the beneficence of belief in reason and individualism, it is impossible to view such ideas with detachment, to divorce the issue of their truth or falsity from the evaluation of them as good or bad. Those who grasp this connection, however, face the occupational hazard of moralism: of treating every intellectual dispute as an occasion for moral condemnation, and finding the odor of depravity in every opponent. In "A Question of Sanction," I warned against this hazard by distinguishing error and evil.

Whether an idea is true or false, and whether it is good or bad, are related issues. But they are distinct, and the issue of truth is primary. The essential characteristic of an idea is its content, the claim it makes about reality. The first and essential question to ask about any idea, therefore, is whether the claim it makes is true or false. Truth or falsity is a feature that an idea has by virtue of its content. An idea is good or bad, by contrast, in virtue of its relation to some action. As I indicated in "A Question of Sanction," there are two categories of relevant action. We can evaluate an idea by its effects—the actions it leads people to take—as measured by the standard of human life. And we can evaluate an idea by the mental actions that produced it, as measured by the standard of rationality. In either case, the value significance of the idea is a derivative property, which depends not only on the content of the idea but on the nature of the relevant action. And in either case, as I said, "the concept of evil applies primarily to actions, and to the people who perform them." It applies only in a derivative way to the ideas themselves.

Thus, for example, when Marxist ideas are implemented, they lead to widespread death and destruction through the actions of tyrants like Stalin. It's because the ideas are false that they produce *these* effects rather than universal brotherhood, peace and prosperity. That is, the truth or falsity of an idea is its essential trait, underlying and explaining its causal powers. Because the effects of Marxist ideas are bad, moreover, we evaluate the ideas as bad. The logical pattern of this evaluation is: death, destruction, and tyranny are bad by the standard of human life; therefore that which causes them is bad.[1] It would be a logical inversion to say: the ideas are bad in themselves, therefore whatever they produce must be bad—as if we couldn't evaluate Stalin's actions until we knew their ideological basis. Had the same actions been committed by an Attila, whose power did not rest on ideological justifications, the actions would have been equally wrong.[2]

Of all the points I made in "A Question of Sanction," none has been so thoroughly discussed, or so often misunderstood, as the distinction between error and evil. Peikoff has interpreted my position as a defense of ivory-tower amoralism, a demand that ideas and intellectuals be exempt from morality. This is a complete distortion. But he is right that my position is quite different from his.

Peikoff accepts the basic approach I have outlined: first determine whether an idea is true or false, then evaluate it by its causes and its consequences. But he goes on to claim that the value significance of an idea follows *directly* from its truth or falsity: "Just as every 'is' implies an 'ought,' so every identification of an idea's truth or falsehood implies *a moral evaluation of the idea and of its advocates.*" The truth or falsity of an idea, he says, "immediately implies" both the kinds of consequences it will have and the rationality of the mental process that led to the idea. In regard to the latter, "truth implies as its cause a virtuous mental process; falsehood, beyond a certain point, implies a process of vice," i.e., evasion and irrationality. Honest errors, especially in regard to philosophical issues, are thus very rare; he suggests that they are essentially limited to the retarded, the illiterate, and the young.[3]

What I object to is the claim that the truth or falsity of an idea has immediate implications about its causes and consequences. Obviously there *is* a connection between truth and positive consequences; otherwise, we would have no reason for seeking the truth. And there is a connection between the rationality of our thinking and the truth of our conclusions; otherwise, we would have no reason to be rational. But these connections are much more complex than Peikoff allows.

As a sign of this complexity, let us observe the contradiction in his view.

Ideas and Original Sin

When we say that an idea has consequences, we are saying that the idea is a *cause* from which certain effects follow through a sequence of necessary steps. In the cases we're concerned with, the sequence begins with the philosophers who originate and develop the idea. When the idea becomes widely accepted in philosophy, it spreads to other disciplines, where thinkers incorporate it into their theories. It then expands into the culture at large through the work of artists, journalists, commentators, and other intellectual retailers, who apply the idea to countless matters of detail. In time it becomes an element in the dominant psychology of an age, predisposing people to accept the kinds of art, behavior, and institutions that are consistent with the idea.

When Peikoff writes of this sequence, he describes it as inexorable. The effect of injecting Kant's ideas into the cultural mainstream, he writes, "has to be mass death." Kant "unleashed" Lenin, Stalin, Hitler "and all the other disasters of our disastrous age. Without the philosophic climate Kant and his intellectual followers created, none of these disasters could have occurred; given that climate, *none could have been averted*."[4] These are very strong claims about historical causation.[5] To say that the process is inexorable, that none of the consequences could have been averted, is to assume that the individuals who serve as links in the causal chain had no choice in the matter. These individuals must, in effect, be helpless and unwitting carriers of the intellectual virus.

This indeed appears to be Peikoff's view. He recognizes that all people, not just philosophical originators, have free will. But he suggests that most people are not in a position to exercise free choice about fundamental philosophical ideas. In an essay on the philosophy of history, he writes: "The vast majority of men never even rise to the point of accepting a philosophy in any way different from the familiar ideas they automatized in growing up." Consequently, "Millions, billions, of men may be oblivious to the mind, they may be ignorant of philosophy, they may even be contemptuous of abstractions. But, knowingly or not, they are shaped ultimately by the abstractions of a small handful of individuals."[6]

If a person is shaped unknowingly by such abstractions, however, he is not responsible for accepting them, and thereby contributing to the causal sequence by which they produce the disasters. If these ideas are so deeply embedded in one's culture, upbringing, and economic and political environment that they never become explicit for the ordinary, non-intellectual person, never become issues about which he can choose whether to think or not to think, then that person cannot be accused of evasion or irrationality for accepting them. Yet in "Fact and Value," Peikoff holds such people responsible. "'The mass base of such [irrational] movements are not evaders of the same kind [as the leaders]; but most of the followers are dishonest in their own passive way. They are unthinking, intellectually irresponsible ballast, unconcerned with logic or truth."[7] And Peikoff is committed to this view by his more general principle that the falsity of an idea "immediately implies" irrationality on the part of those who accept it. If we do hold followers responsible in this way, however, then they are agents and partners in the disasters that result. Those disasters do not then follow inexorably from the ideas, and the philosophers who originated the ideas may be given only a diluted share of the blame for the consequences.

In short, Peikoff cannot have it both ways. Ideas necessitate historical results only to the extent that people do not freely choose all of the intellectual contents that govern their values and behavior. Ideas necessitate results only to the extent that artists, journalists, politicians, and people in other walks of life operate within an intellectual context that they necessarily take for granted. But to this extent, they are not responsible for the effects of the premises that make up that context, and cannot be condemned as irrational. To the extent that people *are* responsible for thinking about their premises, and choosing to accept or reject them, the link between the originators of the ideas and the ultimate consequences is not one of causal necessity. We cannot hold the originators fully responsible for those effects, any more than we can hold a bartender fully responsible for the drunken behavior of his patrons.

Peikoff's view amounts to a cultural version of the doctrine of original sin. The Christian thinkers held that Adam's sin of disobedience to God caused a change in human nature, an inescapable tendency toward greed, concupiscence, pride, and other sins. As descendants of Adam, we inherit this flaw; we have no choice or control over it. Yet it is nevertheless a sin for which theologians said we are responsible and are properly condemned by God. It is this contradiction that Ayn Rand denounced as a "monstrous absurdity."[8] The absurdity consists in passing moral judgment, which presupposes choice, on something that one holds to be necessitated. The same contradiction is present when Peikoff condemns individuals for accepting ideas with vicious consequences. In passing moral judgment, he presupposes that the individuals act freely; in attributing consequences to ideas, he presupposes that the ideas spread ineluctably, like Adam's sin, in a manner not subject to individual choice.

The relationship of an idea to its consequences or its causes, therefore, is *not* one of immediate implication. These relationships are much more complex, especially in the case of the fundamental philosophical ideas where Peikoff holds that the implications are clearest. In the realm of philosophy and culture, we are dealing not with causal necessity but with influences over which individuals exercise varying degrees of partial control. Putting Peikoff's view aside, then, let us look more closely at the nature of these relationships.

The Role of Ideas in History

Ideas have consequences because man has an inescapable need for moral principles. As volitional beings, we need standards for deciding what goals to pursue, and what kinds of actions will achieve them. Since our mode of cognition is conceptual, these standards must take the form of principles: an abstract code of values and virtues. No one can escape the need for a moral code of some kind, even if it is only a haphazard collection of proverbs and rules of thumb. A person's political views, his sense of what is proper in personal conduct, and his sense of his own self-worth depend on the standards of evaluation he has accepted. These standards in turn are shaped by his assumptions about human nature, the purpose of life, the possibility and value of knowledge, the relationship of the individual to society, and other such philosophical issues. It is possible to form independent views on all of these matters. But most people are also influenced by the dominant views in their culture, taking on the philosophical coloration of their social environment.

These facts about individual psychology have a social implication: the ideas of the thinkers who shape a culture will have far-reaching effects on the values and beliefs of the people in a society, and thus on their actions and their social institutions. Since philosophical ideas underlie all others, it is philosophers who set the fundamental direction. Their ideas do indeed have consequences. But this brief summary masks the enormous complexity of the causal relationships involved. A human society is the most intricate phenomenon in nature, with causal relationships at many different levels of organization, interacting in myriad ways. Even in economics, which studies material production and exchange, and which is the closest thing we have to a science of society, fundamental questions remain unsettled: the relevant variables to measure, the relative priority of various causal factors, and the relations among factors at the micro and macro levels. The study of culture, of *intellectual* production and exchange, is in a much more primitive state. The argument summarized above is a sound reason for assigning an important causal role to philosophical ideas. But once we go beyond this broad thesis, we must proceed with caution.

We should note, to begin with, that an idea may have two different kinds of effects. If a person believes in religious faith as a form of knowledge superseding reason, then other things being equal he will rely on faith and not let reason interfere with his belief in God, an afterlife, or whatever. This is a *direct* consequence of the idea. The person is simply acting in accordance with the principle he accepts; his epistemological policy is explicitly contained in and endorsed by the idea. A further consequence is that the person will feel out of control in those areas of his life where he practices faith. He will feel subconsciously that certain things are unknowable, and will experience an undercurrent of anxiety and a loss of self-esteem. This consequence is *indirect*, because it is *not* part of the content of mysticism. It occurs because, mysticism being false, the person who accepts it is not in fact gaining a new mode of knowledge but rather compromising the only real mode of knowledge he has. When we assert this cause-effect relationship, we are not simply reading off the effect from the content of the idea, as we do with direct consequences. We are relying on our own judgment that man needs a sense of mental efficacy and that reason is its only source.

The same distinction applies to the role of ideas in a culture. Modern liberalism holds that the government should regulate the economy and transfer wealth among individuals, mixing freedom and controls by reference to the social good. The existence of regulatory and transfer programs is therefore a direct consequence of this ideology. Since in fact there is no such entity as society apart from the individuals who compose it, nor any social good apart from their good, a further indirect consequence is that the imposition of controls is governed by gang warfare among pressure groups. Liberals (by and large) do not advocate rule by gang warfare. This is not part of the content of their view. The consequence occurs because their view includes a false belief about the nature of society and the good. The effect is a joint result of two factors: the existence of discretionary power in government, which is a direct consequence of liberal ideas; and the fact that individuals and interest groups will compete to use that power in their own interests. This latter is a fact about human nature; it is not a product of liberalism.

The distinction between direct and indirect consequences applies not only to the implementation of ideas in reality, but to the historical evolution of the ideas themselves. One effect of Kant's system was the emergence of philosophical collectivism, because Kant taught that happiness should be sacrificed to duty. Kant himself, however, was not a collectivist. He thought the source of our duties was not society but a higher, "noumenal" self residing within every individual. In acting from a sense of duty, he claimed, we are treating this higher self, in ourselves and in others, as an end in itself. In political philosophy, accordingly, Kant was an individualist, advocating individual rights and a limited government. It was because there is no such thing as the noumenal self that later thinkers such as Hegel, who wanted to preserve the ethics of duty, turned to society as its source and object. Kant's philosophy, then, did contribute to collectivism, but the effect was indirect. To say that Kant "implicitly advocates murder,"[9] as Peikoff seems to do, is to twist the concept of advocacy beyond recognition.

Only the direct effects of an idea are immediately implied by its content, and it is only these effects that exponents of the idea can be said to be advocating. The indirect effects occur because the idea is false. To grasp that such effects do or would follow from implementing the idea, one must first grasp that the idea is false. Until an exponent is prepared to abandon his idea as false, in other words, we cannot expect him to accept our assertion that his ideas have destructive consequences. In attributing such consequences to the idea, we are relying on our own opposing philosophical views. Until he is persuaded of the truth of our views, he will properly reject the attribution of the consequences to his ideas, and will reject as unfair the claim that he advocates those consequences, even implicitly.[10]

Objectivists should be especially sensitive to this point. All of us have heard the accusation that we are fascists, and felt that the charge was a preposterous misinterpretation. The real problem is that the accusers are reading into our defense of egoism their own assumption that egoism involves the sacrifice of others to self and thus the glorification of power. If that assumption were true, then our philosophy would indeed have bad effects. But they would be indirect effects, and our critics would still have to acknowledge that we do not advocate the pursuit of power as such. Fairness requires that we draw the same distinction when we criticize other views.

Whether we are speaking of direct or indirect consequences, moreover, we must recognize that we are using a kind of shorthand when we attribute the effects to the ideas themselves. Strictly speaking, an idea is not a causal agent, because it is not an entity. When we speak of an idea at the cultural level, we are abstracting a common content from the minds of all the people who accept and act upon it. This is a legitimate abstraction; ideas in this sense may be thought of as cultural variables, analogous to the unemployment rate and other macroeconomic variables that economists study. But we must avoid the Keynesian error of reifying these variables and treating them as if they have some causal power independent of the particular people and events from which they are abstracted. Abstractions as such do not exist, and have no effects. When we attribute such large-scale effects as the American Revolution or the Nazi death camps to a set of ideas, we are speaking of a causal chain involving the activities of millions of people over the span of centuries —including not only the originators of the ideas, but all those who promulgate them, who develop and modify them, or who put them into practice. The individuals involved act *as* individuals, not as passive vehicles of an Hegelian spirit that exists apart from them. Without their actions, ideas would have no effect; and the particular nature of the effect depends on the manner in which they exercise their initiative.

To illustrate the point, let us consider once again the ideas of Kant. These ideas had disastrous consequences only because and to the extent that they were, as Peikoff puts it, "injected into the cultural mainstream." But this process of "injection" was not automatic, nor was it a function solely of the content of the ideas. Those ideas would have remained inert, first of all, were they not widely taken up by other intellectuals, and this was partly a function of the wider intellectual context in which Kant's works appeared. The influence of his system was due in large part to the fact that it seemed to provide an escape from a number of philosophical corners into which his Enlightenment predecessors had painted themselves: scepticism about the senses and the validity of induction, the is-ought problem in ethics, the failure to develop an adequate theory of concepts. Had Kant put forward his ideas two centuries earlier, I believe most thinkers would have found them unintelligible, and they would have disappeared into obscurity.

In fact, moreover, Kant's system was not widely accepted in the form in which he left it. It was modified extensively by a long line of thinkers: Hegel, Marx, Schopenhauer, Nietzsche, and others. None of them was of Kant's stature, and none could break out of the context created by his fundamental premises. But within that context, the modifications they introduced were substantial; they involved original acts of thought by powerful minds who freely committed themselves to a lifetime of philosophical work. In retrospect, we can see a certain logic in the way they developed Kant's premises, but that line of development was not causally necessitated, and other developments would have been equally possible. Had a religious thinker of Aquinas' stature appeared in Kant's wake, for example, a return to some sort of Christian mysticism would have been just as consistent with Kant's premises as the emergence of secular collectivism.

Nor is it true that a culture develops monolithically along a single line laid down by a particular set of ideas. In every period there are competing ideas within philosophy and related fields. The outcome of this competition depends on which ideas win the allegiance of the most intelligent and energetic of the non-original thinkers in the universities and other cultural institutions. These thinkers may not contribute fundamentally new ideas, but they do select among available ideas with some degree of autonomy. And they are influenced by factors other than the ideas themselves. The tradition of Kant, Hegel, Marx, *et. al.* led to totalitarian dictatorships in Germany and Russia, but in Western Europe and America the result was welfare-state liberalism, which retained some elements of individualism. Of course that difference may itself be explained by reference to ideas: the individualism of the

Enlightenment had taken stronger hold in these countries, and was embodied in traditions of individual rights, limited government, and the rule of law. But this tradition goes back to the Magna Carta in the thirteenth century, long before the Enlightenment. In other words, the prevalence of certain ideas among the intellectuals of a period depends not only on the internal logic of the ideas themselves, but also on political and other factors that cannot all be traced back to ideas. Otherwise we could not explain why certain ideas are more widely adopted in one country than in another, or why they have such different effects.

To have any effect, finally, an idea must be implemented. It must affect the actions of producers, politicians, and other non-intellectuals. These people, like the second-tier thinkers, select among the ideas available to them in their culture, and the selection is partly determined by factors other than the ideas themselves. One such factor is reality. Ayn Rand observed that "Collectivism—as a political ideal—died in World War II."[11] And we are currently witnessing the death throes of communism as a political system in Eastern Europe, and quite possibly in the Soviet Union. These results occurred not because intellectuals have rejected the philosophical bases of collectivism, but because people have observed its effects with their own eyes. In short, ideas have consequences only in and through the actions of individual people who are not mere passive conduits or unwitting carriers, who are subject to many influences other than ideas, and who exercise some degree of autonomous judgment about the ideas they do accept.

As a result, the consequences of a given idea cannot be inferred directly or solely from its content; and the consequences do not follow inevitably, as a matter of strict causal necessity. An observer at the time of Kant, armed with the knowledge provided by Objectivism, could have predicted that no good could come from these ideas if they became widespread. But he could not have predicted whether they *would* become widely accepted and acted upon. Nor could he have predicted that the results would be mass death in some countries, a welfare state in others.

The role of ideas in a culture is derived from their role in an individual psychology, just as macroeconomics is derived from microeconomics. At the psychological level, the ideas an individual accepts will determine, within broad outlines, his feelings, choices, and actions. But no causal necessity determines which ideas he will accept. That depends on his volitional use of his mind. The same is true for a culture. If a society embraces a set of philosophical ideas; if those ideas are woven into every aspect of its culture, economy, and political institutions; if people routinely appeal to those ideas to explain and justify their actions—then there is no escape from certain consequences, and the philosophical ideas provide the deepest explanation of the society's fate. The ideas prevailing in a given period set fundamental constraints on what is economically, politically, culturally, and intellectually possible. This is why ideas matter. This is why false ideas may properly be opposed out of a commitment to the good as well as to the true.

But it is quite another thing to say that philosophical ideas enact themselves, compelling their own acceptance; or that a culture is a machine that philosophers manipulate by injecting certain fundamental premises. This is a much stronger claim about historical causation. It amounts to a kind of intellectual determinism—preferable to Marx's economic determinism, because ideas are more important than economic factors as causes, but no less objectionable as a form of determinism. I doubt that any of my readers will defend this thesis explicitly. But we must not embrace it implicitly when we assign responsibility for historical events.

I want to comment in this regard on the distinction I drew in "A Question of Sanction" between the Soviet tyrants and the academic Marxist. If we ask who was causally responsible for the mass murders that occurred in Soviet Russia, the answer is: Stalin and those who worked with and for him. The deaths occurred with their knowledge and by their order. These men were the proximate causes of the deaths, and were fully responsible for them. What then was the role of the intellectuals? Together with the antecedent cultural factors that existed in Russia, intellectuals were responsible for creating the conditions in which it was possible for the killers to gain power, and to kill on such a massive scale.

But there's a difference in degree of responsibility. Stalin was personally responsible for the deaths. He did not actually pull the trigger; he had accomplices. But the deaths occurred because of his exercise of political power he possessed as an individual. Had Stalin not existed, the leader who succeeded Lenin might not have been so brutal or killed on so wide a scale. By contrast, no one intellectual is fully responsible for creating the conditions in which a Stalin was possible. The academic Marxist of my example was one voice among countless others; had he not existed, the result would not have been noticeably different, even if no one else took his place. Some critics of "A Question of Sanction" have said that the academic Marxist is guiltier than Stalin, because his ideas were the underlying cause of the horrors. This argument is doubly fallacious: first in attributing causal agency to the ideas themselves, and secondly for investing that agency in every individual adherent of the ideas, treating each one as fully responsible for effects that occurred only because millions of other people embraced the same ideas. This is the kind of irrationality we see in current liability law, where someone marginally responsible for an accident may be sued for the full amount of the damages.

More important, however, there is a difference in the nature of their responsibility. Stalin was a murderer; he intended to kill, and he carried out his intention. His victims had no choice in the matter; he did not have to persuade them to volunteer for immolation. The academic, by contrast, was an exponent of ideas. Even though his ideas were incompatible with man's nature as a rational being, the office he occupied in the causal chain *was* consistent with that fact: he was engaged in persuasion, in the effort to provide reasons for his political views. Even if he was intellectually dishonest,[12] and his views were caused by evasion, his advocacy of Marxism could have an effect only by eliciting the willing assent of his listeners. If we believe in free will, we must assume that they freely endorsed and adopted his position, that his arguments were not causes affecting them willy-nilly. I am not denying that such advocacy is a form of action, as Peikoff seems to think. I am simply noting the difference between two kinds of action: murder and persuasion. Objectivists, of all people, should be alive to that distinction.

If the Marxist were honestly mistaken, finally, and later abandoned his position, he would certainly regret any success he had had as a polemicist for his former beliefs. If his views had been widely known, he would want to make public his change of mind. In the end, however, he would recognize that he is not his brothers' keeper. The audience he had as a Marxist was responsible for weighing the arguments he offered, and agreeing or disagreeing in accordance with their own judgment.

But Peikoff holds that regret is not enough. Such a person must accept *guilt*. Speaking of the young who have been innocently taken in by bad ideas, he says "the best among these young people are contrite; they recognize the aid and comfort, inadvertent though it be, which they have been giving to error and evil, and they seek to make amends for it."[13] The religious language of this passage is a mark of Peikoff's intrinsicism. He is speaking here of people who have been honestly convinced of a doctrine; they have acted in accordance with their own first-hand judgment of the issues. By objective standards they have acted morally. They have not earned any guilt and should not accept it. Only an intrinsicist, who believes that guilt attaches to certain actions regardless of the agent's knowledge or context, would speak of contrition and atonement in such a case.

Peikoff denies, however, that an academic Marxist could be honestly mistaken. To evaluate this claim, we must now examine the relation between ideas and their causes: the mental processes of those who accept them.

The Scope of Honest Error

If we know the consequences of an idea, we may evaluate it in the broad sense discussed in Section I, the sense in which we may evaluate *anything*—from a tidal wave to a piece of legislation—by its effect on human life. I discussed this issue at some length because I believe Objectivists tend to reify ideas as causal agents, and thus to oversimplify their actual causal role. But this is not the main issue in the current controversy. The main issue concerns *moral* judgment. To pass a moral judgment on someone for the ideas he holds, it is not enough merely to evaluate those ideas by their consequences. We must also consider his motive: we must consider whether and to what extent his beliefs are the product of a rational process of thought.

How do we judge a person's innocence or guilt in this respect? Can we make the judgment solely by examining the content of his belief? Can we tell from the truth or falsity of an idea, and from its consequences, whether those who accept it are rational or irrational? This is the central issue on which Peikoff and I disagree. He asserts that the truth or falsity of an idea "immediately implies ... the relation to reality of the mental processes involved." Falsehood must go "beyond a certain point," or reach "a certain scale," before it implies irrationality—qualifications intended to allow for the possibility of honest error. But such errors, he says, "are not nearly so common as some people wish to think, especially in the field of philosophy." His discussion suggests that only a "groping teenager" could innocently be taken in by bad philosophical ideas. Any adult who subscribes to a false philosophical idea must therefore be guilty of evasion and irrationality. And the logic of his basic argument requires this thesis. He cannot justify his contempt for tolerance, or his claim that "every identification of an idea's truth or falsehood implies *a moral evaluation of the idea and of its advocates*," if honest errors are anything more than a rare and insignificant possibility.[14]

Peikoff seems to be saying, in other words, that the acceptance of virtually any philosophical falsehood is proof of irrationality. It should be noted, however, that he puts this thesis forward in the context of a digression concerning "inherently dishonest ideas." Since he does not define this category, one cannot tell whether he thinks it includes all philosophical errors. He has elsewhere spoken of innocent errors; and he presumably agrees with Schwartz's claim that many liberals and conservatives hold mistaken but not necessarily irrational views, even though their views normally have elements of mysticism or subjectivism, altruism or collectivism.[15] The thesis implies, moreover, that virtually anyone who is not an Objectivist is irrational. This in turn implies that any honest person could have arrived at the Objectivist position—despite Peikoff's claim that Objectivism is not just common sense but a revolutionary philosophy that required an extraordinary mind to have discovered it.[16] So it isn't clear exactly what Peikoff believes. Nevertheless, it is important to see why the thesis as I have stated it is false.

I should stress at the outset that I believe we *can* make moral judgments about people in the intellectual sphere. My point is that these judgments do not follow solely from the content of what they believe. We must consider the *how* as well as the *what*: we must consider the way in which they arrived at their conclusions, and the relationship between those conclusions and the rest of their knowledge.

Let us begin by asking why error is possible in the first place. Conceptual thought is fallible because it involves a conscious process of integrating what is given by the senses. Perceptual awareness is not subject to error, because it is automatic. But conceptual thought involves the conscious, self-directed activity of thinking: focusing on common properties in what we perceive, forming abstract concepts and principles, drawing conclusions from evidence. These are voluntary actions. We must choose to initiate the process and to carry it through objectively, without evading any fact or letting subjective biases influence our conclusions. If volition were the only source of error, then Peikoff would be right: any error would imply a voluntary failure to remain objective, for which the person could properly be blamed. But volition is only one aspect of the cognitive process involved in thinking; there are many other ways in which the process can go wrong. Let us consider a few of the more common ones.

Because conceptual thought is conscious, volitional, and self-directed, we need methodological standards to guide us—the canons of inductive and deductive inference, of scientfic method, of classification and definition. These standards are not innate. It took heroic efforts on the part of many great minds to discover them, and it takes a good deal of time and effort for most students to learn them. Even with the best will in the world, it is perfectly possible to commit errors of thinking because one has not fully mastered the relevant skills, or because some complexity in the subject matter makes it difficult to apply the methods properly. This is especially so today, given the abysmal education most people get in logical thinking. Thus a person's thought may be irrational, in the sense of violating a canon of reason, without involving any evasion or other culpable mental lapse.[17]

A proper methodology includes not only the basic techniques of reasoning contained in any logic textbook, but the more advanced techniques that are distinctive to the Objectivist epistemology: observing the contextual and hierarchical nature of knowledge, not multiplying concepts beyond necessity, avoiding rationalism and empiricism. Many of the ideas we oppose are rooted in the failure to observe these standards. Libertarian advocates of competing governments, for example, are usually rationalists who apply a principle (that competition is good, enforced monopoly bad) in a mechanical, deductive way, disregarding its proper context. Such methodological errors *may* involve bad motives. Some people who drop context, or use floating abstractions, or think in nonessential terms, are being willfully nonobjective. But this is not always the case. Precisely because the Objectivist epistemology is new, and its methodological implications not obvious, we cannot assume that everyone who fails to observe these standards is being dishonest.

Another source of innocent errors is a failure to consider all the relevant alternatives. Thinking does not take place in a mental vacuum; we approach any cognitive task with a range of alternatives in mind, and errors can occur when that range is too restricted. The solution to a problem may elude us because it lies outside the range of solutions that normally work with problems of that kind. When we seek to explain someone's behavior, we may settle prematurely on a certain hypothesis because we haven't considered all the other possible explanations. And in philosophy, people often adopt a position on an issue because it seems preferable to the other positions they're familiar with; but the range of positions they consider may be restricted by an underlying assumption that they have not identified and therefore cannot challenge.

In ethics, for example, the standard defense of altruism is that one must either sacrifice oneself to others or others to oneself. The possibility of an egoist theory without sacrifices either way is excluded by the assumption that there are conflicts of interest among people. To challenge that assumption, one must reject the further assumption that interests are subjective, which means one must find the objective basis for interests, which means one must grasp that values derive from man's needs as a living organism with a specific nature. This last was a major insight on Ayn Rand's part, not an obvious point that could be overlooked only by an evader. Similar examples can be found in every branch of philosophy. Indeed, Ayn Rand's distinctive trait as a philosopher was her ability to identify and challenge the deep assumptions that had boxed in her predecessors.

The alternatives we consider are a function of the context of knowledge we bring to a given issue. Our context can lead to errors in other ways as well. We've all had the experience of making innocent errors because we didn't take account of some fact that simply was not available to us at the time. Consider Peikoff's example of the two employees. One comes up with a new idea that will increase profits; the boss rightly infers that he had to initiate a rational process of thought to arrive at the idea, and praises him accordingly. The other offers "a stupid suggestion, which flies in the face of the facts"; the boss concludes that the employee was out of focus, and evaluates him negatively.[18] Peikoff ignores the possibility of intelligent errors: an employee proposes something that won't work because of some subtle factor he was not aware of, but that represents a thoughtful integration of all the other relevant factors. Anyone who has worked with people knows that this is a common occurrence. That's why most of us find discussion with others valuable for our own thinking. Because other people bring different contexts of knowledge (and different kinds of skills) to an issue, they may alert us to facts we hadn't known, or make clear the relevance of facts we hadn't appreciated, or redefine the issue in a way that permits an easier solution.

The same is true in philosophy. With the exception of the axioms, all philosophical knowledge is contextual in the same way as any other kind of knowledge. Consider the basic principle that reason is man's means of survival. Ayn Rand often observed that this principle rests on the evidence provided by the Industrial Revolution. It was obvious to the Greeks that reason is distinctive to man and allows him to live in a way that other animals cannot. But it was not until the modern era that scientific theories developed to the point of being applicable to production. Only then did it become clear that the yield of productive labor could be increased indefinitely; that it was possible to break the cycle of famines and plagues; that an ever-increasing population could survive, at an ever-increasing standard of living, within the same geographical region. Prior to the Industrial Revolution, the true power of reason could not have been appreciated because these facts lay outside the context of human knowledge. And even now, they remain outside an individual's context of knowledge until he has sifted through the historical evidence and identified them as the *central* consequences of the Industrial Revolution, isolating them from all the other changes and dislocations it brought. Given the way history is normally taught in the schools, many individuals never reach this point.

I believe that Objectivists often fail to appreciate the contextual nature of philosophy because they do not appreciate the role of induction. Philosophical principles rest on inductive inference from the concretes of our own experience, our observation of others, and our knowledge of history and nature. We use deductive reasoning to integrate these principles, to check for consistency, and to apply the principles to new concretes. But the principles themselves rest on induction. And the relevant inductive evidence is immense.

The Objectivist ethics, for example, may be reduced to two points: the choice to live, and the law of causality. Once we accept life as our ultimate goal, we discover what it requires by discovering the causal connections between man's nature and his life. Causal connections are established by induction. That reason is man's means of survival; that it is a faculty of the individual; that human life must be supported by production; that a being with a rational and volitional mode of consciousness requires self-esteem; that in virtue of the foregoing, man needs philosophy, art, recreation, friendship and romantic love—these and all the other principles of the Objectivist ethics must be established by inductive evidence regarding human nature.

To accept rationality as a virtue, for example, one must be convinced that there is no inherent conflict between reason and emotion. Yet we do observe such conflicts, in ourselves and others. In order to show that they are not inherent in human nature, we must show that emotions are causally dependent on the results of past thinking—the value premises we have accepted and made automatic. This causal connection is established inductively. It can be illustrated by the kind of simple examples customarily used in the Objectivist literature. But a rational person will not accept these as proof of the generalization. He will want to observe the connection introspectively in his own case, and to do so on a wide enough range of examples to be sure that the principle applies to *all* emotions. This is not an easy task, even for someone with good introspective skills. Since the thesis pertains to all human beings, moreover, a rational person must remain open to non-introspective evidence from psychology, neurobiology, and other sciences. Given the scope and complexity of the relevant evidence, we cannot assume that a person is irrational simply because he does not accept our conclusion.

The inductive nature of philosophy, then, is yet another source of innocent error. Consider once again the issue of altruism. A person growing up in a conventional American town would observe that the decent people tend to subscribe to the conventional altruist ethics, and that to some extent they act accordingly: they "temper" justice with mercy, they give to charity, they are not especially ambitious. He would also observe another class of people who are criticized for being selfish, and who tend to be self-centered, vain, grasping, cold and exploitative. The natural generalization to draw from these data is that the basic choice in life is whether to sacrifice self to others or others to self. It takes a certain degree of intelligence and imagination to see that these are not the only possibilities, that the grasping sort are not in fact acting for their own interests, and that the decent sort act altruistically only because they themselves have accepted the same dichotomy.

It's important in this regard to appreciate the role of history as a body of inductive data, especially for issues in political philosophy. The average person who understands the ethical and economic case for capitalism will nevertheless resist the conclusion so long as he accepts the standard historical view that the Industrial Revolution impoverished the workers, that the great industrialists were robber barons, that laissez-faire capitalism spawned monopolies, and so forth. Such a person is faced with a conflict between a deductive argument for capitalism and an inductive argument against it. It would be rationalistic for him to ignore the inductive data. He would be right to insist that the deductive case be accompanied by historical evidence showing that the standard claims are myths.

In light of these features of conceptual thought—the need for a method, the role of alternatives, the contextual nature of knowledge, and the importance of induction—it is clear that error need not be caused by a willful departure from reality. Honest errors are not a rare and insignificant phenomenon. This is especially true in philosophy, as I have tried to indicate by my examples. There's a natural temptation to treat philosophical principles as self-evident because of their breadth and fundamentality. The temptation is even stronger when the principles are as thoroughly integrated with each other as they are in the Objectivist system. There's a natural temptation to ask why other people can't just *see* that Objectivism is true. But only an intrinsicist could take the question seriously. One cannot literally see the truth of a philosophy. With the exception of the axioms, philosophical principles are *not* self-evident. The very abstractness that gives them their breadth and fundamentality means that the cognitive chain which ties them to reality is extraordinarily long and complex. For all these reasons, the scope of honest error is quite large.

This does not mean that all errors are honest. People subscribe to mistaken views, in philosophy as elsewhere, for any number of bad motives. But it does mean that we cannot judge a person's rationality solely by reference to the content of his ideas. How then do we form such judgments? Peikoff says there is no answer to this question.

> If the content of a man's ideas, even when they are openly at war with reason and reality, does not necessarily indicate a process of evasion on his part, how can we ever know that a man who disagrees with us after a discussion is being irrational? How can we know that he is not merely "honestly mistaken" still? Kelley does not address such questions, because the only answer to them is: on Kelley's premises, one never can know that a man is being irrational and, therefore, one never does pronounce moral judgment.[19]

In fact, however, the reason I did not address these questions is that I thought the answers were obvious.

In judging rationality, we are concerned with the process by which a person arrived at his ideas. We cannot observe this process directly; we cannot literally see an act of thought or evasion in someone else's mind. But the process is revealed in numerous ways—by the kinds of connections a person makes, by his openness to evidence, by his general demeanor. One may observe how a person deals with the objections one raises, how willing he is to examine the issues in depth, to lay out his reasons for his position. One may observe whether a person gets angry when his position is challenged, or relies on the cruder sorts of fallacies such as *ad hominem* or appeal to emotion, or dodges from one issue to another in response to objections. These are all signs of non-objectivity. They tell one that *some* motive is at work other than a desire to grasp the facts. We may also see evidence of specific motives. The way in which a person defends relativism in ethics, for example, may reveal that he is moved by hostility toward the very idea of objective standards, rather than any honest difficulty in seeing the link between facts and values.

These are judgments about the process of thought rather than its product. They must therefore be supported by observing *how* a person thinks, by attending to his reasoning rather than his conclusions in isolation. Peikoff himself seems to recognize this. He says that the false content of a man's ideas indicates evasion if the ideas are "openly at war with reason and reality." The word "openly" turns his statement into a tautology. If a person's departure from the facts is open, i.e., explicit, then of course he is being willfully non-objective. But we can't tell whether this is so merely from the content of his beliefs. Peikoff also adds the qualification that we must judge a person "after a discussion." Why would a discussion be necessary if the ideas themselves directly implied irrationality?

It is not hard to find evidence about another person's process of thought. To form a judgment on the basis of this evidence, however, we must proceed in accordance with the general standards of judgment outlined in Section I. For example, a person who hears a new argument against a long-held view may flounder, resorting to fallacious arguments and otherwise giving evidence of irrationality. But we should not judge him irrational—as a person, or even on the matter in question—until he has had time to reflect on the matter and reach a settled opinion. I have yet to meet the person who has not breached the standards of rationality at one time or another in the heat of argument. One cannot form a judgment without knowing whether such a breach is an aberration or a standing policy. This may take more than the single discussion that Peikoff seems willing to allow. And it requires that we actually listen to the person's reasons, making some effort to understand his position from the inside, rather than granting a *pro forma* hearing, secure in the certainty that he will fail to establish his honesty. A person's process of thought may also be reflected in the way he writes; it is often possible to judge an author's rationality from his works. But this requires that we actually read the work—the text itself, not an excerpt or paraphrase by an opponent. I would have thought this too obvious to mention, had I not met Objectivists who casually denounce Kant as the most evil man in history without having read a word of what he wrote.[20]

Inherently Dishonest Ideas

Anyone who sojourns even briefly in the academic world will have frequent occasion to hold his nose. He will find egalitarians who favor a society in which no one is allowed to earn more than a minimum wage. He will find radical feminists who dream of erasing the biological differences between men and women, and subjecting reproduction to community control. He will find literary critics who believe that texts do not exist apart from readers. He will find scholars who advocate an affirmative action policy toward the canon of great books, ending the "hegemony" of white European males like Shakespeare, Locke, and Newton. He will find old-line Marxists who are disappointed by events in Eastern Europe.

In ninety-nine cases out of a hundred, these views are expressed in a manner that leaves no doubt about the motives behind them. Envy and malice, hostility toward standards of any kind, adolescent glee at the fall of reason—such motives are no longer hidden behind the layers of rationalization that a dim sense of decency used to require. We may assume in advance that proponents of such ideas are overwhelmingly likely to prove irrational. Nevertheless, I would deny that the ideas are inherently dishonest in a literal sense—i.e., that no honest error in thinking could possibly lead someone to embrace them. All of these ideas can be defended by some semi-plausible consideration that normally functions as a rationalization, but that could induce someone to accept the idea through an honest error. In most of these cases, I have actually met such people. In judging an individual, therefore, one cannot go merely by the content of what he believes. Here, as with less noxious ideas, one must have independent evidence about his motives for believing it. Since the bad motives behind these ideas are usually pretty obvious, this is not a taxing requirement.

I believe it is fruitless to define a category of inherently dishonest ideas, and then try to list its members. A more accurate approach would be to rank ideas on a continuum defined by the likelihood that adherents of the idea are honest. At one extreme are issues about which any error is almost certainly innocent. As we move along the continuum, the probability shifts toward the assumption that the error springs from irrationality, and proponents of the ideas must bear an increasingly heavy burden of proving their intellectual honesty. The far end of this continuum is the open rejection of reason as such.

By this I do not mean disagreement with the Objectivist analysis of reason. Someone can honestly believe in scepticism, intrinsicism, or the primacy of consciousness because he does not see how to defend the validity of the senses or the objectivity of conceptual knowledge. It is even possible for an unsophisticated person to believe in telepathy or "channeling" on the basis of the anecdotal "evidence" in supermarket tabloids. These views are distinct from the epistemological nihilism I have in mind: the explicit, wholesale rejection of reason, not in the name of something higher, not out of ignorance of what reason is, not because of difficulties in defending reason, but as an act of sheer negation. I cannot imagine an innocent motive for such nihilism, and I think one may know without further evidence that one is in the presence of evil. In all lesser cases, however, at least some shred of further evidence is required.

These lesser cases include the ideas of altruism, mysticism, and the mind-body dichotomy, and I want to comment in this regard on the works in which Ayn Rand analyzed and condemned the motives behind them. In "Galt's Speech," she traces the entire syndrome to a desire to make whim efficacious. "[T]he purpose for which they dissolve the absolutes of reason, logic, matter, existence, reality," she writes, "is to erect upon that plastic fog a single holy absolute: their *Wish*."[21] In her essay "For the New Intellectual," she lays more stress on the psycho-epistemological roots of such ideas: "It is against this faculty, the faculty of reason, that Attila and the Witch Doctor rebel. The key to both their souls is their longing for the effortless, irresponsible, automatic consciousness of an animal." Both Attila and the Witch Doctor exhibit what she described in her later works as the anti-conceptual mentality: "a consciousness held down to the *perceptual* method of functioning, an awareness that does not extend beyond the automatic, the immediate, the given, the involuntary."[22]

I think these analyses are accurate and profoundly insightful as cultural explanations. They explain why these doctrines have been so appealing to people and have had so firm a grip on our culture, despite the fact that they are false. But this does not mean that her analyses can be used to judge individual exponents of the doctrines, on the assumption that the anti-conceptual mentality and whim-worship are the *only* possible bases for accepting them.

This is simply not true. Each of these ideas can be defended philosophically by plausible though mistaken arguments; each of them has been put forward as a plausible though mistaken solution to a genuine philosophical problem. I have already discussed the case of altruism. Mysticism has been defended by its more philosophical exponents (such as Plato) on the basis of what I call the diaphanous model of consciousness, a view to which virtually every major philosopher (including Aristotle) has subscribed in one form or another.[23] The mind-body dichotomy is rooted in a variety of considerations that might easily lead one to hold that mind and body, consciousness and matter, are utterly distinct and opposed kinds of entities. The philosophical issues with which these doctrines are concerned are not easy ones, and we cannot assume that every adherent of the doctrines is *ipso facto* immoral.

The issues discussed in this section are not philosophical primaries. The relation between ideas and their consequences is an issue in the philosophy of history; the Objectivist theory about this relation rests on a view of society, morality, the nature of concepts, and the hierarchical structure of knowledge. Similarly, the question of how to judge people whose views differ from one's own is an application of general standards of moral judgment, which is itself a subissue within ethics. Nevertheless, these derivative issues lie at the center of the current debate within Objectivism, and they have proved to be extraordinarily divisive. The reason, I believe, is that they have a certain psychological primacy. They have a fundamental bearing on what it means to be an Objectivist, and on how we should relate to non-Objectivists. I will take up these matters in my final section. But first let us complete the discussion of evil and error by considering the question of tolerance.

IV. Toleration

The concept of toleration is used in many different contexts, but its core meaning is to endure, allow, or put up with something. The concept presupposes an object that is tolerated: something wrong, false, threatening, painful, disagreeable—something of negative value significance. And it presupposes an action one forbears from taking against that object. Where no action is possible, tolerance is not an issue. We do not tolerate the law of gravity, even when its consequences are inconvenient. To define toleration in any context, therefore, we must specify the nature of the particular object and action in question.

In regard to ideas, the object is a person with whom we disagree, who holds a conviction we believe to be false. One action we forbear from taking is that of silencing the person coercively, or compelling his assent to our own ideas. This is *political* toleration, or freedom of speech and conscience, which is not at issue here. We are concerned with tolerance as an *ethical* virtue, a way of dealing with people that goes beyond respect for their political rights. In this case, the action we forbear from taking is that of condemning and ostracizing the person. It's important to note that the object of toleration is the person, not the ideas *per se*. Tolerance does not mean refusing to express one's belief that the ideas are false or that their consequences are destructive. These issues are part of the normal content of discussion and debate among people concerned with ideas. Tolerance is a matter of one's policy toward such people as individuals, including one's willingness to engage in discussion with them at all.

The question to be considered now is whether tolerance is a virtue, and if so, why? What role does it play in a rational life? What are its limits? What values does it serve? My answer, in brief is that tolerance has both an ethical and an epistemological basis; it is required by justice and by the nature of objectivity. Let us consider these issues in turn.

Tolerance, Justice, and Benevolence

Tolerance is at root a negative concept; it means not condemning a person solely on the basis of his ideas. This policy is appropriate—it is a matter of simple justice—for the reasons I gave in the previous section. Except in rare cases, we cannot tell that a person is irrational merely from the content of an idea he holds. It would therefore be unjust to condemn him on that basis.

The principles of justice also determine the limits of toleration. Tolerance is not appropriate, as I said in "A Question of Sanction," when a person is willfully irrational. Thus I do not hold, as Peikoff claims, that tolerance means suspending moral judgment in the realm of ideas. It means suspending judgment when we lack sufficient evidence. And we should keep in mind here the distinctions we drew in Section I. We form moral judgments at different levels: we can judge a specific action, a general trait, or a person as a whole. The amount of evidence we need normally increases as we move from one level to the next. The same is true in regard to ideas. We may find that a person is not being rational on a particular occasion, in discussing some particular issue, and we may properly end the discussion for that reason. It takes more evidence to conclude that someone is chronically nonobjective in regard to some issue or kind of issue; in that case we may properly decide that we will not discuss politics, or religion, or whatever with him. It takes a great deal of evidence, finally, to judge that a person is irrational as such, on every subject, and to condemn him accordingly. At each level, tolerance is the appropriate policy when we lack the necessary evidence.

There is no conflict, then, between tolerance and justice. But I do not want to leave the impression that tolerance is merely a negative concept, a grudging sort of patience we exercise in order to avoid hasty judgment. If we lack evidence that a person who disagrees with us is irrational, we must operate on the assumption that he is rational. Tolerance is the positive recognition and acceptance of the needs of a rational being, especially the recognition that rational knowledge is held contextually and acquired by independent thought. A person's philosophical views reflect a lifetime of experience. They are woven into his judgments about people, his understanding of history, his sense of the meaning of his own life. A rational person will not change his mind at the drop of a hat. He will not abandon the grounds he had for a belief in the face of demands by others, or change his mind without a first-hand understanding of the facts that require it.

If we hope to persuade him, we must begin by appreciating these needs. We should make an effort to understand his position from the inside, to locate its essential bases and the conceptual links that lie behind it. We should convey our respect for his independence. And we should convey our own objectivity by making it clear that we are as open to persuasion by the facts as we expect him to be. Discussion among rational people is best conducted as a partnership in discovering the truth, not as combat or indoctrination.

To be tolerant, in short, is to acknowledge the virtue of rationality in others—indeed to value and admire it—even when it is exercised in the service of ideas we believe are false. The negative aspect of toleration is refusing to condemn people for errors that are honest; the positive aspect is valuing their honesty even when it is in error. This policy is required by an ethics of reason, and it is the only policy that has any chance of being effective; here, as elsewhere, the moral is the practical. People of self-esteem do not cave in to high-pressure tactics, nor do they quiver in the face of accusations that they are immoral for believing what they do. They simply dismiss the accuser as a zealot or a crank.

Tolerance and Objectivity

Let us turn now to the epistemological aspect of tolerance, specifically its relationship to certainty. I wrote in "A Question of Sanction" that "Tolerance is not a weak-kneed confession of uncertainty. It is a recognition that certainty is contextual." This claim has been questioned by many who observe that tolerance is normally championed today by the opponents of certainty: skeptics, pragmatists, subjectivists in general. And Peikoff has argued that this is the *only* possible basis for tolerance:

> "Tolerance," as used by Kelley, is a concept (or anti-concept) out of the modern liberals' world-view; it is a further expression of the philosophy of subjectivism; it conveys the notion that one must be fair to one's opponents by means of not judging them, by being "open-minded" and saying, in effect: "Who am I to know? Maybe I have something to learn from this person." The term means, in essence, "fairness through skepticism."[1]

I believe that Peikoff's view is false. Though many liberals do advocate tolerance on sceptical grounds, their position is inconsistent. Scepticism is not a basis for tolerance; objectivity is. To see why, we must consider some fundamental issues in epistemology.

A virtue is a means of achieving values. The function of tolerance as a virtue is to provide a necessary condition for open discussion and debate among rational people. These are the values we achieve by dealing with others tolerantly, as rational beings, in the manner described above. The question is: Why are these valuable? Which theory of knowledge would lead one to regard discussion and debate as epistemological values?

It is clear, to begin with, that they are not values for intrinsicism. An intrinsicist holds that facts are revealed without the need for any self-directed or contextual process of integration. The truth is revealed passively, through intuition, revelation, or reliance on authority. Like perception, conceptual knowledge requires no conscious process, no confirmation or proof, no effort beyond the choice to open one's (mental) eyes. All truths are given, self-evident. So we cannot help grasping the truth, and any failure to do so must be willful. Some intrinsicists, like the Protestant thinkers of the Reformation, held that the truth is accessible to everyone. Others, like their Catholic opponents, held that the truth is revealed only to a few, who must then be accepted as authorities by everyone else. Either way, disagreement must be regarded as a moral failure, a willful refusal to accept the truth, and it may properly be condemned. There is no value to be gained from open discussion, because there is nothing to be learned from it. As a rule, therefore, intrinsicists have been explicit foes of toleration.

By contrast, many secular thinkers have tried to defend toleration on subjectivist grounds. A subjectivist holds not only that truth is not revealed, but that opinions are not constrained by the facts in *any* way, at least in the areas of philosophy, politics, and ethics. All doctrines in these areas are on a par, since none can be evaluated as true or false. Opinions may differ in sophistication, internal complexity, or political "correctness," but the more consistent subjectivists hold that the adoption of any such standard is itself a subjective preference, not required by the facts.

The subjectivist argument for tolerance is that since no opinion is better than any other, we have no reason to prohibit people from believing as they wish. But the argument is invalid, because a subjectivist is in no position to appeal to reason. He may *prefer* a tolerant society in which people are free to express their views and interact peaceably, a society in which open discussion is widely valued and practiced. But he cannot claim that this is anything more than a subjective preference on his part. He has no basis for criticizing a conservative subjectivist, who prefers that people be passive, obedient, and uniform in what they believe. Nor has he any basis for criticizing the nihilistic sort of subjectivism that characterized the New Left, which urged people to act out their political fantasies, shouting down speakers they didn't like and otherwise stifling rational discussion.

To show that discussion and debate are values, one must show that they are means to an end, that they are causally related to a goal that is itself objectively valuable. A subjectivist in ethics does not believe that any value is objective, so whatever purpose he thinks is served by discussion, he leaves it open to an opponent to reject that purpose. And a subjectivist in epistemology does not believe that causal connections can be validated objectively, so no matter what purpose he thinks is served by discussion, he leaves it open to an opponent to claim that that purpose is better served by the opposite policy. Discussion and debate are values only if they are means to the discovery of the truth. To defend toleration, therefore, one must accept the primacy of existence: the recognition that facts exist to be discovered, that opinions *can* be evaluated as true or false—in philosophy or politics no less than in science.

It is commonly said that a free marketplace of ideas is the best way to ensure that the truth will emerge; that diversity of opinion is a value because it counters the partiality of any one perspective on the world; that we can't really understand the basis of our own view without hearing the arguments for opposing views. These arguments have been stated with great eloquence by thinkers from John Milton to John Stuart Mill. They are not based on scepticism; they reflect a belief that there is a world and a truth about it. In my judgment, they rest on an implicit grasp of the fact that knowledge is objective, not intrinsic or subjective.

The objective theory of knowledge recognizes that knowledge is acquired by knowers whose faculties have a specific nature and operate in specific ways. It recognizes in particular that conceptual knowledge is not automatic and self-evident like perception. It requires an active, conscious process of integration. Our knowledge does not consist of isolated atoms in random array. It is a complex structure in which every item—every concept, proposition, inference, and theory—is essentially related to others. And since conceptual knowledge rests on the evidence of the senses, it has a hierarchical structure, in which every item is related to reality through the process of observation, concept-formation, and inference that produced it. We cannot detach our conclusions from that process and check them against some list of intrinsically correct answers.

Reason is essentially an integrating faculty. We acquire knowledge by expanding our context—extensively as we integrate new evidence and apply what we know to new fields, and intensively as we integrate more and more thoroughly the things we already know. A mind that never integrates, a mind that waits passively for illumination, will not acquire knowledge. Nor will a mind that integrates blindly. Integration is a fallible process, in all the ways described in the preceding section. We can insure the objectivity of our conclusions only by taking responsibility for checking the steps in the process of thought that produced them, making sure that our inferences were sound and that we took all the relevant facts into account.

Integration and objectivity, then, are cardinal values in cognition. Integration is the engine of knowledge, and objectivity its governor. The objective case for tolerance is that discussion and debate provide a useful—and in some cases practically indispensable—means of achieving these values.

One reason for this is that integration is inherently selective. To integrate is to unite a body of data into a whole: forming a concept that combines similar units into a new mental unit, drawing a conclusion that integrates a body of evidence, devising a hypothesis that unifies a range of phenomena. In these and other cases, the integrative process must omit those features of the data that are irrelevant or nonessential. Consider as simple a process as forming the concept "chair." We start by grouping together certain objects that are similar to each other and that differ from other objects such as tables. To do this, we must ignore the similarities between a given chair and a table—similarities in color or design, for example—in order to focus on their differences. Then we unite the particular chairs into a concept that represents all chairs. To do this, we must omit the specific measurements of shape and function possessed by those chairs as concretes. We must also ignore their other features: color, material, location in the house, etc.

The same pattern occurs *whenever* we integrate data into a new mental unit. The selectivity of integration is the key to its enormous power. But the results are valid only if we select properly: the data we retain and integrate must in fact be relevant and essential; the data we omit must in fact be irrelevant or nonessential. In the case of a simple concept like "chair," there is little risk of error on this score. The risk increases, however, as our integrations become more complex, as we deal with larger masses of data, more abstract concepts, and a wider context of background knowledge. In such cases it is especially important to look at the data from every angle, examining the alternative ways of classifying the material and the different patterns of logical relationships, before we settle on the proper way to integrate. But the relevant considerations are often so numerous that no one mind is likely to hit upon all of them. And we are subject to what psychologists call "confirmation bias." Since the very purpose of integration is to help us organize and retain the data, we tend to remember most easily the data that confirm our conclusions; data that do not fit fall into the penumbra of memory and awareness. Discussion with other people who have integrated things differently, who have attended to different features and patterns in the data, is a way of countering the problem.

Suppose you are thinking about a movie you've seen. To interpret the movie as a work of art, you try to identify the plot, isolating the essential structure of events. You think about statements in the movie that seem to identify the theme explicitly, asking yourself what it was about the context or the formulation that made this statement stand out. You think about the characters: how fully were they developed? what was their essential motivation? which ones succeeded, and which failed? As you reach conclusions about any of these points, your conclusions organize the data. Those elements of the movie that illustrate and support your interpretation stand out; the other elements recede into the background. Your thought is necessarily selective in this way. You cannot hold in mind every moment in the film and every aspect of every scene. Your conclusions are valid only to the extent that the elements you disregard are in fact nonessential, but the tendency to disregard them makes it easy to skip this step in the process and focus only on the supporting data. Discussing the movie with someone who interprets it differently is a useful corrective. A different interpretation will highlight different elements in the film; it will force you to defend your implicit judgment that they are nonessential, and thus provide a check on the objectivity of your conclusions.

Interpreting a movie is not a simple cognitive operation, but it is far simpler than validating a philosophical principle. As I observed in the preceding section, such principles rest on a vast inductive basis, which includes all of our own experience, our knowledge of history, and the data provided by more specialized branches of knowledge such as psychology or economics. To handle this immense body of information, we must be ruthlessly selective—and we must exert special care to avoid the risks of selectivity. To defend our position, we must stand ready to defend our implicit judgments that certain data are essential, others nonessential, and so we must remain open to data that we may have disregarded in haste. We must also beware that a philosophical thesis, like the interpretation of a movie, tends to highlight the data that confirm it, and cast all other data to the periphery of our minds. I do not see how the danger of partiality and hasty integration can be avoided by someone unwilling to debate adherents of other positions. And the danger is greatest for those who integrate with the most vigor and facility. Bright lights cast dark shadows when they shine from one side only.

The objective case for tolerance also rests on the fact that integration serves the purpose Ayn Rand described as unit economy.[2] A mass of data is reduced to a single new unit that may thereafter be retained and used as a unit, and may serve in turn as a datum in a further process of integration. The new mental unit—a concept, conclusion, or theory—is formed by a process that involves conscious attention to the logical relationships among the elements it unites. If the new unit is to function *as* a unit, however, the integrative process on which it is based must be made automatic. The scope of conscious attention is very limited. We cannot use the new unit in further integrative thinking until its logical basis—the similarities that led us to form a concept, the evidence that justifies the conclusion or theory—has been made subconscious.

When its basis is subconscious, the integration is experienced as self-evident; it comes to have the immediacy of direct perception; we take it as obvious. But it is not self-evident, and objectivity requires that we stand ready to check every step in the cognitive process that produced it—to "check our premises," as Ayn Rand often put it. There is thus a psychological tension between integration and objectivity. To integrate, we must make certain concepts and connections automatic, in order to achieve the benefits of unit economy. To be objective, we must be ready to do—automate when necessary.

This takes mental time and effort that we understandably resist. It is always difficult, and can be painful or threatening, to call in question something we took to be fixed. It is so much easier to ignore the new evidence that raises such a question, to say: "I've already settled that issue, I've heard that point before, I know what I know, don't bother me." When we hear a new objection to our philosophy, it is so much easier to slam the system down upon it, dismissing it with the first argument that comes to mind. The best defense against this tendency is a willingness to engage in discussion and debate with those who disagree with us.

For all the reasons I've given, then, the objective theory of knowledge implies that tolerance is a virtue. To understand and validate a particular way of integrating the data in any field, we must consider the alternative ways in which it could be integrated and we must be able to show that ours is better. As John Stuart Mill put it, "He who knows only his own side of the case, knows little of that."[3] Given the selectivity of conceptual knowledge, and the role of automatization, there is no realistic way of meeting this standard without the discipline of debate with live opponents. This policy underlies the adversary system in law. Each party is allowed to integrate fully and freely, making the most powerful and comprehensive case it can for its position. Objectivity is secured by the fact that each side must answer the arguments of the other, and the evidence it cites must stand up to cross-examination by its opponent. The system is not without flaws, but no better system has ever been devised for sifting the facts more carefully. The institutions of peer review and organized debate serve the same function in the sciences and other academic disciplines.

It is true that thinking is not a collective activity. The primary tools of cognition are observation, abstraction, and inference—processes that take place in the privacy of an individual mind. Discussion and debate are secondary tools that provide us with material to integrate and a way of checking the objectivity of our results. The use of these secondary tools must be decided by reference to the primary ones. There's a time to seek opposing views, and a time to decide one has heard enough. A physicist may reasonably forgo the opportunity of debating a Flat Earther. A philosopher may reasonably dismiss the tabloids' latest "evidence" for life after death. For this reason, the cognitive case for tolerance is narrower than the argument from justice. You may have nothing to learn from an opponent if you've heard all his arguments before, yet you may still regard him as honestly mistaken, and so refrain from condemning him.

I also want to emphasize that the argument I have presented is *not* the fundamental argument for freedom of thought and speech. These rights are grounded in the fact that the primary tools of cognition are actions of an individual mind and must be initiated and directed by voluntary choice. By analogy, it would be wrong to cite the benefits of economic competition as the basis for economic freedom. Such freedom is required by the individual's need to dispose of his own productive efforts in the service of his life. But just as competition in the economic marketplace is an inestimable value in the creation of wealth, so open discussion and debate— competition in the marketplace of ideas—are inestimable values in the creation of knowledge. Since tolerance is a necessary condition for these activities, it is an important virtue.

As a final qualification, let us note that the exchange of views is valuable to a rational person only when it takes place within a rational context. Lawyers on opposite sides of a case must accept the framework of legal precedent and rules of evidence. Scientists debating a new theory operate within the context of established fact and the canons of scientific method. Any process of thought rests on substantive assumptions, and proceeds in accordance with some method. But these assumptions and methods are not self-evident. Except for the axioms of philosophy and logic, the principles, assumptions, and rules we employ must be validated. And here, as elsewhere, the exchange of views can be valuable. It is therefore appropriate for legal theorists to debate principles that lawyers must take for granted. It is appropriate for a philosopher who defends the objectivity of science to consider the objections of a sceptic. And even though I consider Kant's epistemology a self-contradictory system that subverts reason at its base, I have learned an immense amount about the real nature of reason by debating Kantians. I could say the same for Marxists in politics.

By way of conclusion, let me stress again that the argument I have offered does not in any way imply or presuppose scepticism, as Peikoff alleges. There is no conflict between tolerance and certainty. A conclusion is certain if it is proven beyond a reasonable doubt; the conclusion must integrate all the available evidence, and the available evidence must rule out the possibility of any other conclusion. Because certainty is a relation between an individual mind and reality, it does not depend epistemologically on any commerce with one's fellows. For all the reasons I have stated, however, such commerce is a psychological necessity—at least in regard to the sorts of complex issues we're concerned with. To know that a conclusion integrates all the available evidence, one must know that he has made all the relevant evidence available to himself and drawn out its implications properly. To know that no other conclusion is consistent with the evidence, he must know that he has considered the relevant alternatives. Our assurance on this score rests partly on the knowledge that we have been open to the insights of our opponents, and fairly met their objections.

"No wise man ever acquired his wisdom in any mode but this," wrote Mill,

> nor is it in the nature of human intellect to become wise in any other manner. The steady habit of correcting and completing his own opinion by collating with those of others, so far from causing doubt and hesitation in carrying it into practice, is the only stable foundation for a just reliance on it: for, being cognisant of all that can, at least obviously, be said against him, and having taken up his position against all gainsayers—knowing that he has sought for objections and difficulties, instead of avoiding them, and has shut out no light which can be thrown upon the subject from any quarter—he has a right to think his judgment better than that of any person, or any multitude, who have not gone through a similar process.[4]

Certainty is possible, in other words, but it is contextual, and on a matter of any complexity, that context is partly social.[5] Those who advocate intolerance in the name of certainty are cutting themselves off from the only basis on which genuine certainty is possible.

V. Objectivism

We have now examined all the major substantive issues I raised in "A Question of Sanction": the standards of moral judgment and sanction, the relation between error and evil, the propriety of tolerance. I have laid out my position on all these matters in a systematic way, and revealed the intrinsicism that runs systematically through the views of my opponents. But we are not quite through.

In "A Question of Sanction," I said that while Objectivism is a magnificent system of ideas, it is not a closed system. I made this point in passing, as a comment about the value of tolerance. But it has become an issue in its own right. Peikoff claims that Objectivism *is* closed; it is "'rigid,' 'narrow,' 'intolerant,' and 'closed-minded.'" He claims that those who disagree with him about the primary issues in this debate should not call themselves Objectivists. In the name of "quality-control," he urges that they leave the movement or be driven out.[1]

The issue he has raised concerns the nature of philosophy as such. But what exactly is the issue? What does it mean to say that a system of ideas is open or closed? These are metaphorical terms. What is their literal content?

A philosophy is a body of principles that add up to a fundamental and distinctive view of reality and of man's place in it. In order to give us a *fundamental* view, a philosophy must address a broad range of issues in metaphysics, epistemology, ethics, and other areas, and do so in a systematic way. This is what distinguishes a philosophical system from an isolated philosophical position in a particular area, such as egoism in ethics. In order to give us a *distinctive* view of reality and man, moreover, a philosophy must take a definite position on the issue it addresses, a position different from that of other philosophies. A system that tried to embrace every viewpoint, in a spirit of ecumenism, would not be a philosophy; it would be a vague and contradictory hash.

A body of principles does not exist apart from the individual minds who grasp them. Knowledge presupposes a knower, an "ism" requires an "ist." A philosophy defines a school of thought, a category of thinkers who subscribe to the same principles. In an open philosophy, members of the school may differ among themselves over many issues within the framework of the basic principles they accept. Those issues include a vast array of detailed questions in every area of philosophy, as well as the proper formulation of the basic principles themselves and their interrelationships. Over time, moreover, the philosophy develops. It grows and expands, in the way a science does, as thinkers build on the work of their predecessors. Of course there must be limits on the process if the system is to retain its identity. A system cannot embrace every point of view, nor can it develop into its opposite. In an open system, however, these limits are set by fundamental principles: the system is defined by the essential tenets that distinguish it from other viewpoints. A closed system, by contrast, is defined by specific articles of faith, usually laid out in some canonical text. Internal debates are highly constrained and usually short-lived; they are typically settled by a ruling from some authority.

Peikoff denies that Objectivism—or indeed any philosophy—is an open system. "Every philosophy," he says, "is immutable. New implications, applications, integrations can always be discovered; but the essence of the system—its fundamental principles and their consequences in every branch—is laid down once and for all by the philosophy's author." In the case of Objectivism, of course, the author is Ayn Rand, and the philosophy is defined by an "official, authorized doctrine" contained in her works. Peikoff seems to allow that some further development of her ideas is possible, as long as it is "logically consistent with what she wrote." *Atlas Shrugged* and her other writings are to Objectivism, he says, what the Constitution is to the legal system of the United States. A judge must accept the entire Constitution and make sure that his decisions are consistent with every sentence in it; an Objectivist, presumably, must take the same approach to Ayn Rand's texts.[2]

Peikoff is saying, in other words, that the philosophy is closed in the sense of being *complete*: nothing essential may be added to the system, which was laid down "once and for all" by Ayn Rand. Future developments will consist only of new "implications, applications, integrations"— a list from which the term "discoveries" is conspicuously absent. And he regards Objectivism as closed in the sense of having a highly specific *identity*: as a philosophy, it includes every philosophical belief she expressed; as a school of thought, it excludes anyone who disagrees on any point. In sum, Objectivism is nothing less, and not much more, than the content of her works.

These extraordinary claims have no precedent and no foundation. The historic systems of philosophy, as distinct from religions and totalitarian ideologies, do not exhibit the features he ascribes to Objectivism. Nor are those features consistent with the content of Ayn Rand's philosophy, especially her theory of knowledge. Peikoff's view of Objectivism as a closed system is yet another expression of intrinsicism. And its practical import is an essentially tribal view of the movement, an attitude that breeds insularity and authoritarianism. In this section I will support this assessment of his claims, and present an alternative view of Objectivism as an open philosophy and movement.

Open and Closed Systems

It has been said that Western history is a battle between the followers of Plato and Aristotle. The great, all-encompassing debate in philosophy is between those who accept and those who deny the existence of a world beyond this one; and their champions are Plato and Aristotle. Plato believed in a realm of ideal timeless perfection, which lies beyond this perceivable world of matter and change, and which we can grasp only through a mystical transcendence of the senses. He regarded man as torn by warring elements—a body mired in this world and a soul yearning for the other—and therefore propounded an ethics of renunciation, to free the soul from earthly desires. Aristotle is the quintessential this-worldly philosopher. He denied that there is any world beyond the one we live in, the world of nature, the world we perceive with our senses and understand by reason. He rejected Plato's mysticism. He held that there is no necessary conflict between mind and body or reason and emotion. Man in his view is an integrated being who should seek his happiness in this life, and may hope to achieve it.

What I have described in these broad terms are the two philosophical tendencies we refer to as Platonism and Aristotelians. Perhaps it is this level of generality that Peikoff has in mind when he says that the fundamental principles of a philosophy are "laid down once and for all by the philosophy's author." In these two cases, the philosophical tendency, the broad vision, *did* spring from the genius of a single mind. But this is not always so. Ayn Rand identified a third broad tendency: the materialist, subjectivist, relativist approach that she represented by the symbol of Attila.[3] This philosophical system had many exponents, from the Sophists of ancient Greece to Karl Marx and a host of other thinkers in our own era, but it did not spring from a single author of the stature of Plato or Aristotle.

In any case, if this is the level at which Peikoff claims that a philosophical system is closed in the sense of being complete, he is certainly wrong in his claim about its identity. The systems I have mentioned have had many exponents in addition to Plato and Aristotle themselves, and within each camp there have been many variants. Platonists have argued with themselves, and with Plato, over issues that fall under each of the points in my description. The same is true of Aristotelians and materialists.

Medieval culture, for example, is properly described as Platonist, even though St. Augustine and the other Church Fathers transformed Plato's world of Forms into a heaven occupied by a personal God—a view that Plato himself would not have accepted. Similarly, the Aristotelian seed that Thomas Aquinas planted in the 13th century had its fullest flowering in the Enlightenment. But when we describe the Enlightenment as an Aristotelian age, we must remember that we are abstracting from a great many differences among the thinkers of the time. Many of them did not regard Aristotle as the source of their ideas, and of those who did, none would have regarded Aristotle's work as a founding document with which his own ideas had to be squared.

In our own era, the most influential system is that of Immanuel Kant, whose ideas have also gone through a great many permutations. There have in fact been very few orthodox Kantians. Most people use this term to refer to ideas that share Kant's basic epistemological view about the relation of mind to reality, or his ethical view about the relation between values and duty. Objectivists typically use the term even more broadly, to refer to virtually all our opponents: positivists and pragmatists, Freudians and behaviorists, existentialists, linguistic analysts, the entire gamut of unreason. Many of these thinkers would not agree with a word Kant wrote.

Kant's philosophy, moreover, was instrumental in the growth of modern collectivism, because of his view that reason is inefficacious and his ethical theory that we must subordinate our personal interests and happiness to duty. Most Objectivists, myself included, would say that collectivism is the political expression of Kantianism. But Kant himself was an individualist. He was a classical liberal who believed that individuals have rights, that they are ends in themselves who may not be used for social purposes. Here is a case in which the consequences of a system for an entire branch of philosophy are the exact opposite of those laid down by its author.

The philosophies I've cited are the broadest of all the historical systems. I mentioned them not only because they provide the most obvious evidence against Peikoff's claims, but also because Plato, Aristotle, and Kant are the turning points, the prime philosophical movers, in Western culture. There have been many lesser systems, such as those of Locke and Descartes, which were built around insights of lesser scope, or combined elements of the broader traditions. These systems would be more narrowly defined, because they are not distinct from one another on so fundamental a level as the epochal systems. Further along this same continuum are thinkers like F. H. Bradley and Arthur Schopenhauer, whose systems were merely variants of idealism, distinguished by relatively nonessential points. At the end of the spectrum, and really outside the realm of philosophy, are doctrines like Christianity and Marxism-Leninism. These systems have founding documents that are regarded as canonical. They have well-developed orthodoxies to which adherents are expected to swear allegiance. Each had an institution—the Church and the Party, respectively—that defined the orthodox interpretation of the system and ruled on who can be admitted to the ranks of the believers. Christianity and Marxism come closest to fitting Peikoff's description of a philosophical system. But neither of them is the kind of system that Objectivism aspires to be.

Objectivism as an Open System

Ayn Rand broke new ground in every branch of philosophy; her insights exposed and challenged the deepest assumptions of her predecessors. Because she understood the importance of integration, she was a self-conscious "system-builder": her views of reality, of knowledge, of human nature, of values, and of society form an integrated whole. As a result, Objectivism is an original and distinctive philosophical system, and I think it will prove to be of historic importance.

The perennial conflict in philosophy, as I have said, is between this-worldly and other-worldly philosophers. In the ancient world, this battle was fought primarily in metaphysics. In the modern era, it has been recast in epistemological terms, with Kant as the modern Platonist. Instead of a metaphysical dichotomy between a world of matter and a world of Forms, Kant instituted a dichotomy between appearance and reality. The natural world, he claimed, is apparent only; reality lies beyond, inaccessible to our senses and our reason. For Kant, as for Plato, man is torn between warring elements: a superficial self moved by natural desires and interests, and a deeper self—the real self—which seeks moral perfection through obedience to absolute duties. Ayn Rand cut through these dichotomies. Her concept of objectivity eliminates the breach between appearance and reality: the object of knowledge is the world itself as it appears to a knower with our faculties. Her theory of rational egoism eliminates the breach between interest and idealism: our happiness is to be achieved by fidelity to moral absolutes that are grounded in man's nature as a living being. In time, I think her system will come to be seen as the fundamental alternative to Kant's, in the way that Aristotle was a fundamental alternative to Plato.

But I am speaking of a potential that has not yet been realized. Kant laid out his system in enormous detail, in volume after volume. The same is true of Plato, Aristotle, and other great systematic philosophers. Ayn Rand did not develop her ideas in the form of detailed treatises. Her philosophical essays, as distinct from her fiction and her cultural and political commentary, would fit comfortably in a single volume.[4] A philosophical system must address a wide range of specific issues—the classical problems of philosophy that arise in every branch. The great historical systems met this standard. It cannot be met in a single volume, no matter how brilliant. And of course Objectivism is a young philosophy; it hasn't had two hundred years, much less two thousand, for scholars to play out all the possible variations, to sift and explore the ideas, to develop their consequences. By historical standards, what we have is no more (though no less) than the foundation and outline of a system.

In epistemology, for example, the one issue that Ayn Rand dealt with in detail was the nature of concepts and universals. Her *Introduction to Objectivist Epistemology* is comparable in its systematic character to the writings of Aristotle or Locke on this question. Beyond a brief suggestion, however, she wrote nothing about the nature of propositions, an issue that is essential for a viable theory of truth. In regard to the senses, her distinction between what we perceive and the form in which we perceive it is the key that solves the traditional puzzles of perception, but using the key is not a trivial matter; a great many subordinate questions must be answered to formulate and validate the distinction properly. Ayn Rand identified the fact that knowledge is hierarchical and contextual, insights that I have relied upon throughout this essay and that point to the solution of many traditional problems in epistemology. But a pointer is not a solution. Objectivism does not yet have well-developed answers to such questions as what constitutes proof or how to draw the line between the arbitrary and the false. Nor does it have an adequate theory of induction and scientific explanation.

An analysis of other areas in philosophy would reveal the same pattern: great insights that are partially developed in some directions, not at all in others. If Objectivism is to survive and flourish as a system of thought, it must attract philosophers who will build on Ayn Rand's discoveries, using them as a base for an assault on specific problems in philosophy and drawing out their implications for other disciplines such as economics, psychology, and literary theory. And Objectivism is more than a theoretical structure; it is a philosophy to live by. Over time, the accumulated experience of those who practice it will produce a moral tradition, a body of reflection about the issues that arise in applying the principles. As this happens, the philosophic content of Objectivism will become more complex and detailed. Philosophers who specialize in various fields will address issues that Ayn Rand did not consider, and put forward ideas that were not hers.

This will not be a matter of adding blocks to a monolithic structure, with everyone in full agreement at every step. People will disagree about the proper approach to a given problem and the merits of proposed solutions. New insights and connections at this level will also lead thinkers to modify points that they previously took as settled. They may find it necessary to reformulate principles, or qualify them, or reconceive the hierarchical relations among them. And any such modification will of course be a subject of debate. All of this is part of the process of inquiry. It has been part of the brief history of Objectivism to date, and it is to be expected in light of the Objectivist theory that knowledge is contextual. When Ayn Rand urged us to check our premises, she never exempted her own.

The greatest contributions to this development will come from the most rational and independent minds, whose only concern is the truth. They will not function with double vision, as Peikoff demands, keeping one eye on reality and the other on Ayn Rand's texts. This approach would be inconsistent with any philosophy of reason. It is especially deadly for a philosophy that has so much potential yet to be realized. An Objectivist thinker must be a thinker first, an Objectivist second. He must regard Ayn Rand as he regards any great mind from whom he has learned: he gives her credit for her discoveries, and admires her accordingly, but admits no obligation to accept her as an authority. Peikoff's view that Objectivism has an authorized doctrine leaves us with two alternatives. We may treat consistency with her writings as a value to be achieved at all costs, trimming our mental sails to ensure that result. Or we may remain loyal to our perception of the facts and be prepared to announce that we are not Objectivists, should we find ourselves in disagreement with even the least fundamental of her philosophical ideas. To be Objectivists, in other words, we must abandon rationality; to be rational, we must be ready at any moment to abandon Objectivism.[5]

This point alone is enough to discredit Peikoff's account of the philosophy. But let us pursue the matter one step further, by examining his arguments. Philosophy, he says, is immutable: "it does not change with the growth of human knowledge."[6] Why not? One reason he offers is that philosophy "deals only with the kinds of issues available to men in any era." This is a half-truth. The issues are "available" only in the sense that the relevant facts can be grasped without specialized research. But it is intrinsicism to think that these facts reveal themselves diaphanously. An enormous intellectual context is required to form the necessary concepts, to ask the right questions, to appreciate the significance of the facts. This context is *not* available to men in every era. The concept of individual rights, for example, is required and validated by facts that the ancient Greeks could have observed, but even Aristotle did not form the concept. It took a long sequence of intellectual development, which was not complete until the seventeenth century, before thinkers could grasp the principle of rights.

Peikoff also argues that philosophy does not change with the growth of knowledge because "it is the base and precondition of that growth."[7] This is less than a half-truth, since it is true only of the axioms. An axiom is a self-evident principle that is implicit in all knowledge. Once it is grasped, it is not subject to further confirmation, qualification, or revision in light of new evidence, because it defines the standards by which evidence is used. Apart from the axioms, however, philosophical principles are not self-evident; and while they serve to integrate the rest of our knowledge, they do not provide its base in the way the axioms do. On the contrary, such principles rest inductively on the very body of knowledge which they integrate and explain. As a result, these principles are not acontextual; they are not evidentially closed. By the very nature of inductive knowledge, they are subject to further confirmation, qualification, or revision.[8]

If someone claimed to have evidence against the law of non-contradiction, we could be sure in advance that the evidence is mistaken. If that law is not an absolute, then there is no such thing as evidence, truth, or facts. One cannot claim to know that a principle presupposed by any possible knowledge is false. Suppose, by contrast, that we found certain concepts to which the theory of measurement-omission seemed inapplicable. Here we could not take the same approach. Because the theory explains so much, we would not give it up lightly. We would first try to show that the evidence is mistaken. But we could not be certain of this in advance, as we were with the law of non-contradiction. As an inductive hypothesis about the functioning of a natural object—the human mind— the theory of measurement-omission is open to the possibility of revision in the same way that Newton's theory of gravity was. And the same is true for the other principles of Objectivism.

Peikoff seems to deny this possibility when he says that "a proper philosophy is an integrated whole, any change in any element of which would destroy the entire system."[9] But genuine knowledge is not so brittle. Newton's discoveries were preserved within the broader context of Einstein's theory, even though they were modified to take account of factors that Newton was not aware of. In the same way, a philosophical conclusion that is consistent with everything we know may need revision to take account of new considerations as they arise. But in philosophy as in science, these revisions do not destroy our prior knowledge; they expand and enrich it.

There is also a subtle form of intrinsicism in Peikoff's claim. A philosophy is an integrated whole, as he says. So is any form of conceptual knowledge—science, history, mathematics, or whatever. In every case, the logical relationships among the elements are essential to their meaning and validation. But these connections are not revealed. They must be discovered by a process of thought, they must be held contextually, and they are subject to debate. Suppose an Objectivist philosopher disagrees with Ayn Rand on some particular point. This does not necessarily mean that he rejects her view on all the other principles to which the point in question is logically related. It may well be that he takes the position he does because he regards it as the true implication of those principles. If we disagree with him, we must be prepared to *prove* him wrong. We cannot assume in advance, without argument, that his alteration would "destroy the system" merely because it is an alteration. A case in point is the present controversy. In regard to the scope of honest error, for example, both Peikoff and I appeal to the basic principles of Objectivism in defense of our respective positions, and both of us argue that the other's position is not compatible with those principles. Even if it could be shown—and I do not think it can be shown—that Ayn Rand would take Peikoff's side on this issue, the question would remain: which position is in fact consistent with the basic principles of Objectivism? That question must be decided by logic, not authority.

This brings us to a final argument for Objectivism as a closed system, an argument that lies close to the surface in Peikoff's essay and has been put forward explicitly by some Objectivists. The argument is that Ayn Rand's relationship to the philosophy is the same as her relationship to her literary works: she is the author of Objectivism in the same sense that she is the author of *Atlas Shrugged*. She is accordingly free to stipulate the content of the term. Objectivism includes all and only the philosophical doctrines she embraced, and the system was closed with her death. No one may add to these doctrines, or abandon or revise any of them, and still call himself an Objectivist—just as no one can alter the content of her novels. The attempt to do so, some might add, is like the efforts of the mediocrities in *The Fountainhead* who claimed the right to disfigure Roark's buildings.

This view is radically mistaken. A literary work is a creation, the concrete embodiment of an idea by a specific author. A philosophy, by contrast, is a body of theoretical knowledge about reality. That is why, as Ayn Rand herself pointed out, a philosophical discovery cannot be copyrighted.[10] The discovery itself, as distinct from a specific text in which it is conveyed, is not the property of the discoverer. Property must be concrete, but a philosophy is a viewpoint that may be held by an open-ended number of people. Moreover, as a body of knowledge, a grasp of certain facts in reality, its content is determined by the nature of those facts, including their relationships and implications, not by anyone's stipulation. Had Ayn Rand omitted the character of Francisco d'Anconia from *Atlas Shrugged*, no one would be free to invent that character and rewrite the novel without her permission, even if such a revision would represent an improvement. But had she died before she discovered that rights may be violated only by physical force, and had someone else discovered this principle, it would have to be included in Objectivism. The system demands it; the issue of who discovered it is irrelevant.[11]

The implication of everything I've said is that if Objectivism is to be regarded as a philosophy rather than a body of dogma, it cannot be defined in the manner Peikoff demands. The alternative is not, as he claims, the freedom to rewrite Objectivism as one wishes. The alternative is to define it objectively. He himself observes that the essence of a philosophy consists in its fundamental principles. Ayn Rand said a great many things, not all of them fundamental. Even if we restrict our attention to her philosophical statements (which is itself an act of interpretation), we will find that they cover a wide range, from the general to the specific, from the fundamental to the derivative. We need to discriminate among them. We need to ask: What is distinctive about Objectivism? At what key points does it differ from other philosophies? What are the essential principles that give it its internal structure as a system? What are the broad avenues that we keep returning to as we make our way through the philosophy?

An analysis of this kind is a delicate scholarly task. It requires extensive knowledge not only of Objectivism, but also of the other systems from which it must be distinguished. A vast number of considerations must guide one's judgment about whether to include or exclude a given principle. In this context, I cannot lay out all these considerations. Nevertheless, I want to indicate which principles I do include, in order to make it clear what I have in mind when I speak of an Objectivist movement.

What Is Objectivism?

In *The Objectivist Newsletter*, Ayn Rand described the central tenets of her philosophy as follows:

> In *metaphysics*, that reality exists as an objective absolute;
> In *epistemology*, that reason is man's only means of perceiving reality and his only means of survival;
> In *ethics*, that man is an end in himself, with the pursuit of his own life, happiness, and self-interest as his highest end;
> In *politics*, laissez-faire capitalism.[12]

Is this the essence of Objectivism? Certainly these four principles are essential. But they are not enough. These are extremely broad doctrines as stated. Every one of them has been defended by other philosophers, and the package as a whole is not too far from the views of many Enlightenment thinkers. If Ayn Rand had said no more than this, we could not credit her with having created a distinctive system, much less a system that provides *the* fundamental alternative to Kant. She would properly be regarded as a secular and individualist thinker within the Aristotelian tradition. To identify what makes Objectivism unique, we have to be more specific. We need to identify the basic insights and connections that allowed Ayn Rand to give an original defense of the four principles I stated. So let us take a closer look at each of the relevant areas.

In metaphysics, Ayn Rand's view of reality as objective, her view of facts as absolutes, is basically Aristotelian. But her formulation of this view states its essential elements with unprecedented depth and clarity. Her axiom of existence expresses the insight that existence is the primary metaphysical fact, not to be questioned or explained; that the question "Why is there something rather than nothing?" is meaningless; that existence does not derive from some more fundamental stratum of forms or essences. Her principle of the primacy of existence denies that reality is malleable by consciousness, even a divine consciousness. This closes off the possibility that nature has a supernatural creator—a possibility that Aristotle left open. And it distinguishes her from modern Kantian views which claim that the world we know is merely an appearance, shaped by our own concepts and conventions. Finally, she formulated the laws of identity and causality as axioms that define the realm of metaphysical facts, and that ground the operations of reason. The law of identity, which says that a thing must have a specific and non-contradictory nature, is the basis for all deductive reasoning. The law of causality, which says that a thing must act in accordance with its nature, is the basis of all inductive reasoning.

In epistemology, Ayn Rand also agreed with Aristotle—up to a point. She held that reason is man's means of knowledge, that it gives us the capacity to grasp the world as it is, that the material of knowledge is provided by the senses, that the method of reason is logic, and that this method is grounded in fact. But she went far beyond this. I would say that three of her insights in epistemology are essential to Objectivism.

The first is her concept of objectivity, and her rejection of the false dichotomy between intrinsicism and subjectivism. I described this insight at the beginning of my essay, and have relied upon it throughout. It runs through every part of her epistemology, as well as her ethics and politics; it is the Archimedean point from which she overthrows the Kantian system. A second and closely related insight is her recognition that reason is the faculty of concepts, and that a concept is an integration of particulars on the basis of their similarities. A concept is an abstraction. It is not merely a name for an arbitrary collection of things we happen to classify together, but an integration of them into a new mental unit that expands the range of our knowledge. An abstraction, however, does not exist as such, over and above the concretes it integrates; it is the rule by which they are integrated. So it cannot be divorced from its perceptual basis and allowed to float free. As a result of this theory, Objectivism has a highly distinctive view about what it means to think conceptually, to think in principles—a view that avoids the classic defects of rationalism on the one hand and empiricism on the other.

The final point I would mention in epistemology is that reason is a volitional faculty: that conceptual integration, unlike sense-perception, is a cognitive function that must be initiated and directed by choice. This is the essence of our free will and the source of our need for epistemological standards. It is also the psychological source of hostility toward reason. In analyzing the varieties of irrationalism, as I noted in Section III, Ayn Rand always traced them back to the desire for an effortless, automatic mode of cognition.

This brings us to the fields of ethics and politics, where Ayn Rand's views were most distinctive. Her most important contribution in ethics is clearly her insight that values are rooted in the phenomenon of life. Values exist because the existence of a living organism depends on its own goal-directed action; in order to survive it must treat certain things as good for it and other things as bad. This is her solution to the notorious is-ought problem in philosophy, the problem of how normative conclusions can be derived from facts about the world, and it provides the basis for an objective ethics.

If we value life, then our nature requires certain kinds of actions, which we identify as virtues. Since reason is our basic means of survival, the primary, essential virtue is rationality: the acceptance of reason as an absolute, a commitment to the use of rational standards and methods in every issue we confront. All of the other virtues are implicit in rationality; they involve the acceptance and use of reason in specific areas such as judging others (justice) or creating value (productiveness). But the virtue of independence deserves special mention because it also involves the recognition and acceptance of the volitional character of reason. The fact that we must initiate and direct the process of thought means that we must not subordinate our judgment of the facts to the minds of others, no matter how numerous; and that the sense of efficacy that is crucial to self-esteem is ours to achieve by our own effort. In this respect, the virtue of independence is the key link between epistemology and politics. Because reason is volitional, it is a faculty of the individual, whose freedom to act independently, on his own autonomous judgment, must be protected by a system of political rights.

If these are the central *virtues* in Objectivism, what are the central *values*? Life, of course, is the fundamental value, but what about the subsidiary values, the ones we need if we are to maintain, fulfill, and enjoy our lives? What is most distinctive to Ayn Rand in this regard is her view about the central role of production in man's life. Productive work, the creation of value, is our basic means of dealing with reality and a precondition for the pursuit of any other value. Psychologically, it is a vital source of one's sense of efficacy and self-worth. Production is not merely a practical necessity; it is man's glory. Our ability to reshape the world in the image of our values, in a world open to our achievement, is the essence of her view of man as a heroic being, a view that shaped and colored everything she wrote.

Finally, we cannot omit her explicit rejection of altruism and the mind-body dichotomy. This is a negative point, but we need to include it because Ayn Rand was virtually without precedent here. Many other philosophers have adopted views that are implicitly egoistic, but few were willing to put their cards on the table, to say explicitly: altruism is wrong, self-sacrifice is a perversion of ethics. The same is true of the dichotomy between mind and body, between the material and the spiritual. Ayn Rand is distinctive in her exalted, idealistic defense of such worldly values as sex and wealth.

In politics, the essence of the Objectivist view is the principle of individual rights. The rights of the individual, not the welfare of the collective, provide the moral basis of capitalism. Of course, Ayn Rand did not originate the concept of rights; she inherited it from the individualist thinkers of the Enlightenment. Her contribution was to give their political individualism an ethical basis in egoism, the right of each individual to pursue his own happiness; and an epistemological basis in the fact that reason is a faculty of the individual mind. She also identified the fact that rights can be violated only by force. A right is a right to action, not to a good like food, shelter, or medical care, and it can be violated only if someone forcibly prevents one from acting. The political implication of these views is that the government must be strictly limited: limited in function to the protection of rights, and limited in its methods to acting in accordance with objective law.

Such, in briefest outline, is the essential content of Objectivism as a philosophy. Not all of the ideas I've mentioned were discovered by Ayn Rand, but many of them were, and the integration of them into a system was hers. This outline captures the essential principles that distinguish Objectivism from every other viewpoint—no adherent of a rival philosophy would embrace all of them. Conversely, anyone who accepted all of these ideas would have to consider himself an Objectivist. But notice what I have left out. I omitted a number of points in epistemology, ethics, and politics. I omitted the entire field of aesthetics, just as Ayn Rand did in her brief summary. I haven't said anything about the role of philosophy in history, or the identification of Kant as an arch-villain.

I've omitted these things, not because I disagree with them, or because they are unimportant, but because they are not primary. Some are technical theories required to explain and defend the primary claims that I did include. Some are implications and applications of those primary claims. All of them are principles of limited range and significance for the system as a whole. They are logically connected to the points I've mentioned, and they contribute to the richness and power of Objectivism as a system of thought; if we regard them as true, we will naturally include them as elements in the system. But someone may challenge these noncentral tenets without ceasing to be an Objectivist. The outline I gave was not intended as an exhaustive presentation of Objectivism as I understand it. My purpose was to identify the boundaries of the debate and development that may take place within Objectivism as a school of thought.

It's also important to stress that the principles I have mentioned are not to be taken as a list of articles of faith. They are elements in a connected system. I have been asked whether I would consider someone to be an Objectivist if he accepted all these principles but denied some other point—e.g., that honesty is a virtue. My answer is that the question is premature. I would need to know the reason for his position. If he rejects honesty because he doesn't like it, even though he happens to like the points I've mentioned, then he would not be an adherent of the Objectivist philosophy because he is not an adherent of *any* philosophy. A philosophy is a logically integrated system, not a grab bag of isolated tenets adopted arbitrarily. If the person did have a reason for his position, then I would need to know what it is. I cannot imagine any argument in favor of dishonesty that does not rest on a rejection of rationality, in which case the person is outside the framework of Objectivism. But if his position is that honesty, while good, is not important enough as an issue to be considered a cardinal virtue; or that the scope of legitimate "white lies" is larger than Ayn Rand allowed; or any number of other variant positions—in all such cases, I would consider him an Objectivist even if I disagreed with him, as long as he defends his view by reference to the basic principles.[13]

Like any other philosophy, in short, Objectivism has an essential core: a set of basic doctrines that distinguishes it from other viewpoints and serves as the skeleton of the system. The implication is that anyone in substantial agreement with those doctrines is an Objectivist. I believe that a great deal of damage has been done by refusing to take this attitude. It's been thirty years since *Atlas Shrugged* was published, the length of an entire generation. After all that time, only a handful of philosophers are willing to identify themselves as Objectivists, and our output has been pretty thin; a complete bibliography would not amount to much. This is partly because Objectivism lies so far outside the mainstream of academic thought. But another reason is the insistence on defining Objectivism in the narrow fashion that Peikoff urges, and the atmosphere of dogmatism that accompanies it. In the name of preserving the purity and integrity of the system, Objectivists have too often relied on stereotypical formulations of Ayn Rand's ideas. They have been quick to pounce on thinkers who might have been their allies. They have greeted new extensions of the system with a timid caution that reminds me of the Council of Scholars in *Anthem*, who spent fifty years debating the wisdom of accepting that radical innovation, the candle. These policies have discouraged independent thinking, they have driven away creative minds, they have kept Objectivism from being the living, growing philosophy it could be.

The Objectivist Movement

The attitudes I have described are part of a larger pattern that has characterized the Objectivist movement throughout its brief history. A great deal has been written about this pattern, and I have no wish to swell the literature. I am neither an historian nor a sociologist. But we need to examine the pattern briefly because it represents the embodiment in practice of the theoretical view that the philosophy is closed.

An intellectual movement is a widescale phenomenon, involving a great many individuals, operating across a span of time and across an entire culture. In this sense it is obviously premature to call Objectivism a movement. But given our aspirations, it is worth dwelling for a moment on the characteristics of movements in general. In a particular discipline of knowledge, a movement involves many individual thinkers who share a common methodology and a common framework, but who work within that framework, exploring new connections among the ideas and extending their reach to new areas. For all the reasons I have stated, this activity requires open discussion and debate. Within the wider cultural arena, the impulse of the ideas flows through thousands of channels: literature and other forms of art, journalism and commentary, educational reform, political activism.

This activity cannot be planned and directed by a central authority, just as economic activity cannot be so planned. The issues are too complex, the cognitive needs and perspectives of the people involved are too diverse. What we have instead is a marketplace of ideas. Competition is as healthy for the production and exchange of ideas as it is for the production and exchange of material goods. So a real movement will not have a single leader. At any given time there will be a number of individuals who distinguish themselves by their work. There will be a dense network of personal relationships and organized groups. There will be rivalries and coalitions. There will be fallings-out. That's the way a movement works.

But it's not the way Objectivism has worked. The Objectivist movement has exhibited certain features that have led some people to describe it as a cult. That term is not accurate: in the literal sense, a cult is based on a religious or other nonrational doctrine, which is clearly not the case with Objectivism. A more accurate term for the phenomenon in question is "tribalism." I use this term in Ayn Rand's sense, to refer to a social and psychological syndrome that can attach to any set of ideas, even rational ones. The tribal person experiences his own identity as dependent on membership in the tribe. He feels that without the group he would be lost, he would not be the person he is, he would not recognize himself. He tends to seek friendships within the tribe, because it is only with other members that he can have a sense of shared identity. He tends to shun outsiders, viewing them with suspicion and hostility. Loyalty to the group is a cardinal value, and it is maintained partly by a sense of "Us against Them." A tribalist fears nothing more than expulsion from the group. That represents a metaphysical threat, the loss of self. So he tends to avoid questioning or disagreeing with the leaders of the group over any issue where expulsion is a real possibility. Indeed, he tends to rely on those leaders generally in deciding what to think, what to do. He substitutes authority for his own independent judgment.

Within the Objectivist movement, a tribal element has long been at war with a rational one. The rational element is a real and important side of the movement. Objectivism has been a positive and liberating influence for many people. It has set them free to develop their talents, realize their dreams, achieve their happiness. But I think it's clear to any objective observer that there is a tribal element as well.

Objectivism is a philosophy of benevolence. It sees the world as an open sunlit field, where success is the norm, where we can approach others with the expectation that they will be rational. And many Objectivists have this attitude. But there's also a darker streak in the movement. Many Objectivists seem shut off from the world, profoundly alienated, seeking friends only among other Objectivists, regarding outsiders with suspicion. They speak freely of the enemies of Objectivism, often with a paranoid sense that the world is scheming to destroy us. They suspect that anyone who succeeds outside the movement must have sold his soul, as in Peikoff's dark allusion to those who "have one foot ... in the Objectivist world and the rest of themselves planted firmly in the conventional world."[14] Objectivist publications have been largely negative in content, filled with horror-file items rather than positive contributions to knowledge. Objectivists sometimes seem to take perverse pleasure in contemplating the awfulness of their enemies. And some have acquired a zest for moral condemnation, an act that benevolent people experience as the occasion for sadness and disappointment.

Again, Objectivism is a philosophy of independence, but within the movement there has always been a certain pressure for conformity in thought and action. When people join an ideological group out of an antecedent and independent belief in its ideas, one expects to find agreement in basic outlook. One does not expect the degree of uniformity—down to matters of personal dress and style, aesthetic preferences, beliefs about political strategy or sexual psychology—that characterized the Objectivist movement, especially in its earlier days. Such conformity was produced in part by a fear of moral condemnation for deviant attitudes or values, a fear that was not without foundation. And in part it was produced by a willingness to substitute authority for independent judgment. In my experience it was not uncommon, especially during the various purges and schisms, to hear explicit appeals to authority: "If Ayn Rand says that so-and-so is a rotter, then he must be; could the author of *Atlas Shrugged* be wrong about it?"

One of the arresting things about Howard Roark, the hero of *The Fountainhead*, is his contempt for cliques, status-seekers, gossip, social hierarchies and social climbing, and all the behavior of courtiers and yes-men. Yet the Objectivist movement has always had an inner circle, an extremely well-defined hierarchy whose members are ranked as much by loyalty as by merit. Many are contemptuous and condescending toward those below them, fearful and fawning toward those above. With a few notable exceptions they have not produced much original work. In "Fact and Value," Peikoff refers to those who do "drift away from Ayn Rand's orbit."[15] The context suggests he thinks it better to remain in her orbit. The striking thing is his metaphor, the image of planets moving passively in the gravitational field of the sun—some nearer, some farther, but all revolving around the center. This is not an image one associates with Roark.

The roots of tribalism, as Ayn Rand explained, are psycho-epistemological; a failure to achieve a fully conceptual mode of functioning.

> The anti-conceptual mentality takes most things as irreducible primaries and regards them as "self-evident." It treats concepts as if they were (memorized) percepts; it treats abstractions as if they were *perceptual* concretes.

A person who functions in this way "can cope only with men who are bound by the same concretes." Because his ideas and values are not based on a rational process of conceptual integration, he has no method of applying them, and must rely on tradition or authority; for the same reason, he must regard anyone with different ideas or values as a threat. The anti-conceptual mind is thus dependent on the group.

> The basic commandment of all such groups, which takes precedence over any other rules, is: *loyalty to the group*—not to ideas, but to people; not to the group's beliefs, which are minimal and chiefly ritualistic, but to the group's members and leaders.[16]

Given the concrete-bound nature of the tribalist, the common bonds that unite most tribes are concrete: race or ethnicity, family membership, a common workplace or occupation, residence in a neighborhood, region, or nation. But there are also intellectual tribes that form around original and charismatic thinkers like Marx or Freud.

Though their beliefs are not "minimal and chiefly ritualistic," these groups have the features of more primitive tribes: a feeling of shared identity, an embattled sense of hostility toward outsiders, an emphasis on loyalty to the group, and especially to its leader. But certain other features are peculiar to intellectual tribes. They derive from the fact that the abstract doctrines uniting the group are treated as perceptual concretes.

One such feature is a demand for ideological purity, and the expulsion of those who question or modify any point in the original doctrine. The distinction between essential and nonessential, between the fundamental and the derivative, applies to abstractions; it does not apply to concretes. Concretes are what they are; they are all equally real. A concrete-bound mind therefore has great difficulty with this distinction. When such a mind espouses an abstract doctrine, it treats every element in the doctrine as equally important, and any challenge as equally threatening.[17] Hence the demand for purity—a demand to which Peikoff gives voice in the conclusion of his essay.

Invoking his authority as Ayn Rand's "intellectual and legal heir," he urges those who disagree with him to banish themselves:

> . . . . please drop out of our movement: drop Ayn Rand, leave Objectivism alone. We do not want you . . . . It is perhaps too early for there to be a mass movement of Objectivists. But let those of us who *are* Objectivists at least make sure that what we are spreading is Ayn Rand's actual ideas, not some distorted hash of them. Let us make sure that in the quest for a national following we are not subverting the integrity of the philosophy to which we are dedicated.[18]

Notice that Peikoff is concerned, not with spreading the truth, but with spreading Ayn Rand's actual ideas; this is his criterion for the integrity of the philosophy. The attitude is typical of an intellectual tribe. As a result, such tribes are characterized by constant purges and schisms; Objectivism has been far from unique in this regard.

A second feature is a certain method of dealing with dissent. The anti-conceptual mentality is intrinsicist: it regards concepts and principles as self-evident, as if they were concretes that could be perceived directly, without the need for integration. Any dissent, accordingly, must be a kind of blindness, a perceptual defect that is not to be answered by arguments but explained by appeal to causes. And every tribal doctrine contains a theory designed to provide such an explanation. Marxists dismissed the objections of their opponents as expressions of bourgeois class interest. Freudians interpreted all criticism as a sign of unconscious psychological problems. These self-protective mechanisms insulate the doctrine from any challenge or counter-evidence, producing a closed system of belief. Ultimately they insulate the doctrine from evidence altogether; they are fundamentally irrational. This is why the issue of the scope of honest error has a vital significance for Objectivism. If we assume in advance that anyone who rejects our ideas must be irrational, we have started down the path that turned Marxism and Freudianism into secular religions.[19]

All of the tribal features I've mentioned have been countered to some extent by the rational content of the philosophy, and by the many benevolent, independent, rational, nondogmatic, fully conceptual minds it has attracted. All of these features, moreover, have been identified and denounced by the leaders of the movement during various periods of reform. As a result, the Objectivist movement has never had the fully tribal, anti-conceptual character of the other doctrines I have cited. It has been the intellectual equivalent of a mixed economy. But another tribal feature has never been addressed, and the failure to do so has undercut every effort at reform. This final trait—the saddest to write of—is the deification of the founder.

Ayn Rand deserves admiration for her achievements, for her independence of mind, for her courage in staying true to her vision through a firestorm of public abuse. She deserves gratitude for the knowledge she gave us. The difference between a rational school of thought and an intellectual tribe is an attitude that goes beyond such admiration and gratitude. A tribe regards the ideas uniting its members as embodied in some unique form in its founder, so that the founder's person and actions have a transcendent kind of value, his assertions have a kind of authority transcending the method used to support them, and attacks on him represent a transcendent form, the very depths, of evil. This attitude was described by religious thinkers as idolatry, or worshipping the concrete symbol in place of what it represents, and Ayn Rand has been its object. For many Objectivists, the truth, the power, the grandeur, the overriding importance of her ideas became vested in her as a person—and, through connection with her, in certain other individuals and organizations—as if there were no distinction between the abstract philosophy and these particular concretes.

The various breaks and excommunications provide the most striking illustration of this problem. Every case with which I am familiar involved some action that was regarded as an insult or injury to Ayn Rand as a person. These actions took place in the context of complex personal or business relationships, the details of which were often not known to those who joined in the condemnations, demonizing the offender as they had deified Ayn Rand. In many cases the actions had no bearing on the person's commitment to the philosophy, yet he was denounced as an enemy of Objectivism and no further reference could be made to his ideas or writings. In this way, personal conflicts were elevated to the status of public issues.

These episodes had an air of moral hysteria about them. The standards of moral judgment I described in Section I were routinely violated: little effort was made to hear the other side of the story; the worst possible motives were attributed without considering any alternative explanations; the person's prior record of achievement was ignored or explained away. The degree of animus against these offenders often seemed out of all proportion to the alleged offense. And I knew people who were more upset at what they thought was done to Ayn Rand than they would have been were it done to themselves. They seethed with borrowed anger. In the most violent of these episodes, that of Nathaniel Branden, the real nature of the wrong he did Ayn Rand was not even known to most of those who denounced him as a moral monster.

The most damaging aspect of idolatry is the feeling that any flaw in Ayn Rand as a person means a flaw in the philosophy, with the implication that any evidence of such flaws is metaphysically threatening. In effect (to paraphrase Dostoyevsky), people felt that if Ayn Rand is not perfect, then everything is permitted. I'm convinced that this explains some of the virulence of the reaction to Barbara Branden's book.[20]

It is clear to me that Ayn Rand was a woman of remarkable integrity, who largely embodied the virtues she espoused. But it is also clear that she had certain other traits often found in great minds who have waged a lonely battle for their ideas: a tendency to surround herself with acolytes from whom she demanded declarations of agreement and loyalty; a growing sense of bitter isolation from the world; a quickness to anger at criticism; a tendency to judge people harshly and in haste. These faults did not outweigh her virtues; I consider them of minor significance in themselves. But they were real, and I thought Branden's book, whatever its other shortcomings, gave a reasonably fair and perceptive account of them.

All of this is arguable, of course. But it should have been argued, and it wasn't. When the book appeared, I was shocked by the refusal of many prominent Objectivists to discuss the issues it raised, and their tendency to condemn anyone who did. Peter Schwartz spent most of his review attacking Branden's credibility by impugning her motives, but then concluded that it didn't matter if the events in the book had actually occurred, since Ayn Rand should be judged by her works.[21] Leonard Peikoff said that in deciding what to think of the book you should ask yourself: "What do *you* believe is possible to a man—or a woman? What kind of soul do *you* think it takes to write *Atlas Shrugged*? And what do you want to see in a historic figure?"[22] The common denominator of these arguments is their indifference to the truth. And the truth in this case was of special importance.

The Passion of Ayn Rand appeared at a time when the Objectivist movement was trying to rid itself of moralism and judgmentalism, trying to restore a sense of openness, spontaneity, and benevolence. This was the theme of Peikoff's lecture series "Understanding Objectivism," and a frequent topic of discussion among Objectivists. To deal with these problems, however, we had to know their source. I do not believe that Ayn Rand herself was entirely responsible for the tribal character of the movement. Whatever role her personality played, it was surely amplified by the aims and fears of her followers. To assume a priori, however, that she had nothing to do with these problems was an act of bad faith on the part of those who professed a desire for reform.

Peikoff in particular has blinked in the face of this final recognition, and in recoil from it has now reversed the positive trend he helped initiate. This, I think, is the real meaning of "Fact and Value." The contradictions and equivocations I have pointed out at length reflect an effort to read Ayn Rand's personality into her philosophy, to twist the principles of Objectivism into a rationalization for her flaws. In the name of objectivity and a commitment to values, he is demanding that we emulate the touchy and intolerant moralism of her worst moments.

If the Objectivist movement is to have a future, it must reject this demand and all the other tribal policies to which it leads. As Ayn Rand said, "a proper association is united by ideas, not by men, and its members are loyal to the ideas, not to the group."[23] Objectivism is first and foremost a philosophy. Anyone who subscribes to the philosophy is an Objectivist, and anyone who works to realize its intellectual, political, or cultural potential is a part of the Objectivist movement—regardless of his relationship or personal history with any particular individual or group. Let us abandon the notion of a central authority with the power to define an orthodoxy and expel dissenters. As long as we think in such terms, what we are thinking about is not a movement but a tribe.

Since our ideas are founded on reason, let us make sure that we associate on terms consistent with the needs and standards of rationality. Rational knowledge is acquired by integrating the facts, by sifting and weighing the evidence, and a vital part of this process is open discussion and debate. We should encourage this process. Rationality means integrity, a loyalty to the conclusions of one's own mind. We should honor this, even in a person whose conclusions we disagree with. Rationality requires justice, adhering strictly to the facts in judging other people, and applying moral standards impartially. We should practice this. And a rational person is independent. Above all, as I said in "A Question of Sanction," let's encourage this virtue within our own ranks. Let us welcome dissent, and the restless ways of the explorers among us.

These are the policies appropriate to an open system, a philosophy of reason.

Postscript

2019

As a work of philosophy, *Truth and Toleration* addresses issues that are broad, fundamental, and timeless. From the moment that human beings acquired the capacity to think in moral principles, they have had to employ some standards and procedures of moral judgment. As societies emerged, ideas have been an important shaping force in culture. And within any society at a given time, partisans of such ideas have had to define the terms on which they associate with those who agree, forming religious, political, artistic, and philosophical movements; and to decide whether and how to tolerate those who disagree.

As a polemical work, however, *Truth and Toleration* was written for a particular context: the Objectivist movement at a crisis point in its development. In the 30 years since the essay was first published, a great deal has changed in the movement and in the world around us. It would take a much longer work to chronicle these changes fully. I can mention here only the ones that bear most directly on the themes of this work.

The Early Years

In 1990, along with the first edition of *Truth and Toleration,* I founded The Atlas Society (TAS) with the help, and for the benefit, of Objectivists who wanted a more open, tolerant, and independent alternative to the orthodox movement led by the Ayn Rand Institute (ARI). But the latter was the only organized game in town—and the only face of Objectivism that the rest of the world saw.

In *Truth and Toleration,* I made the philosophical case that Objectivism is a body of principles—not dogma—which every individual must learn, interpret, and apply for himself. I argued that open discussion and debate—without pressure to conform or fear of moral condemnation for disagreement—are vital to the growth, and indeed survival, of Objectivism. At the time, however, there were no actual institutions attempting to put these philosophical principles and intellectual approach into effect. There was no experience to show that they could be practiced consistently—no inductive proof that what is moral in this respect is also practical. That was not a foregone conclusion.

The Objectivist movement, I held, must remain open to new extensions, refinements, and critiques of its principles in order to grow, yet it must remain true to its basic principles in order to retain its identity. It must keep its doors open to new people who do not fully understand or embrace its ideas, yet still maintain, proudly and publicly, the system of ideas that unites its members as a community. It must engage in civil debate with its opponents, and avoid irrational zealotry, without losing its passion as a cause or its commitment to victory over error and injustice. Yet at the time it was not a certainty that such balancing acts could be carried off without reverting to authoritarianism on the one hand or, on the other hand, becoming an ecumenical, "feel-good" movement that stands for nothing.

Within the first ten years, we proved that that the balance is indeed possible to maintain. Our organization grew rapidly, offering conferences, student programs, and a steady stream of books, pamphlets, and audiotapes of public lectures, with editorial standards that allowed debate but kept our commitment to the essential tenets of Objectivism. And a larger movement grew around us: Independent Objectivists launched their own publications, Internet discussion lists, websites, local societies, summer camps, and other ventures. Together we formed a new community that is still growing in size and developing its own traditions and practices.

In short, we fostered an independent Objectivist movement as a credible alternative to the orthodox one. That's quite an achievement.

A second major achievement was to diminish the ill-will that once existed between libertarians and Objectivists. Libertarians welcomed an independent Objectivist movement in which they were invited to participate. From the outset, many prominent libertarian writers and activists wrote for our publications, spoke at our events, and collaborated in other ways. As an early example, TAS and the Cato Institute co-sponsored a 1997 conference to celebrate the 40th anniversary of the publication of *Atlas Shrugged,* with presentations by a broad range of libertarian and Objectivist leaders. It was a major public acknowledgement of the role that Rand's ideas played in the crusade for capitalism—an acknowledgement carried home by hundreds of participants and covered extensively by the media.

The Atlas Society and the Ayn Rand Institute

Since those early years, The Atlas Society has continued to produce articles on philosophy, cultural commentary, and personal applications of Objectivism, along with educational material, videos, and audio lectures. Altogether they occupy thousands of pages on our website. During the financial crisis of 2007-2009, sales of *Atlas Shrugged* soared over 500,000 as people saw its prophetic relevance, and TAS speakers and writers helped explain the connection. We consulted on the scripts for John Aglialoro's three-part film adaptation of the novel and helped promote it with premieres and commentary. TAS spokesmen have appeared in virtually every major media outlet. Under current CEO Jennifer Grossman, we have taken advantage of new media and new formats. At our birth in 1990, the World Wide Web was still but a gleam in the eye of Tim Berners-Lee. We now have the most successful results on social media among comparable organizations—with comments, shares and likes of our content on the TAS Facebook page outperforming peers by many multiples of engagement. The Ayn Rand Institute has also accomplished a great deal. It has consistently amassed larger budgets, increased its staff, and leveraged sole access to Ayn Rand's copyrighted work, promoting her literature in schools through essay contests and free book distribution. Thanks to ARI's efforts, hundreds of thousands of students had access to Ayn Rand's novels and ideas.

From the beginning, however, ARI and TAS have been in conflict. The conflict is not merely the usual competition among thinkers in the marketplace of ideas, or competition among rival organizations for funding and influence. Among most organizations promoting similar ideas and agendas, such competition is accompanied by friendly cooperation in various ways. That is certainly true of libertarian organizations; and it has always been true of our relationships with them. It is not true of TAS and ARI. From the very beginning, we have been the target of moral condemnation as well as intellectual disagreement. To be fair, my attribution of tribalism to orthodox Objectivists is no less morally freighted. I was replying in kind to a moral attack. But it didn't stop there. For years, ARI's leaders and allied groups have denounced us morally as "enemies of Objectivism." ARI has prohibited its campus groups from inviting speakers associated with TAS. And, until recently,

ARI scholars did not reference previous work by our scholars (including older works of mine that, before the break, were welcomed as contributions to the philosophy).

That was then. What about now? In the near-term perspective, there have been changes in leadership in both organizations. As of this writing, principals are talking across the divide and some efforts to collaborate have begun. In the longer term, I am mindful that the breaks and schisms in the Objectivist movement are not unique to Objectivism. They have occurred in many other intellectual movements. The conflicts within Freudian psychology and Marxism are particularly well-known examples in the history of ideas. There are others.

These episodes tend to follow a pattern; they have what I call a natural history (the term biologists use for field observations of species and their life-cycles) that has happened many times in other movements. A brilliant, innovative, charismatic thinker originates a system of ideas that excite and energize people, who flock to the thinker to study at his or her feet. Some stay as disciples to help advance and promote the new theory. A network is formed, the nucleus of a movement. But at some point the inner circle is ruptured by personal conflicts, or a new line of thought that the originator doesn't approve. Some disciples stay with the founder, with a new insistence on protecting the integrity of the system; others form rival parties within the movement, or leave the movement.

In this first generation of followers, the intellectual conflicts are typically infused with personal animosity. There are accusations of betrayal and immorality. People refuse to speak across party lines. But with succeeding generations, the personal animosity attenuates, and with it the high moral dudgeon. And then the ideas can stand on their own—the broad system as a whole, and the interpretations and innovations that individual thinkers put forward. They stand or fall by their merit as ideas, without the external props of sanction or authority. That's what I envision for this conflict, in good time.

Are we there? No. Whether we get there depends on the rationality of Objectivist leaders, present and future, and on their willingness to discuss the issues in a rational and civil manner.

The Issues

The issues are the most important thing—the only important thing, really. So where do we stand?

On libertarianism, the first issue broached in *Truth and Toleration*, I can be brief. ARI and its followers have essentially accepted the view that I argued for in 1990 and that TAS adopted as a policy from the beginning. As I mentioned above, we made it one of our first priorities to heal breaches with the libertarian movement, especially with its premier organizations: Cato Institute, Reason Foundation, Institute for Humane Studies, Competitive Enterprise Institute, Atlas Network, and many others. ARI at the time, like Rand, denounced libertarians, and denounced me for dealing with them, as I have described. By the mid-2000s, however, ARI was collaborating with many of these organizations. In 2013, John Allison even became CEO of Cato.

ARI's online explanation begins by affirming Peter Schwartz's claim that libertarianism is nihilistic (in his 1985 article "Libertarianism: The Perversion of Liberty") which I critiqued in Chapter 2. We haven't changed our view, they say. It is libertarianism—and the meaning of the word "libertarian"—that have changed.[1] The explanation is casuistic; ARI has obviously changed its policy and now follows the path we blazed long ago. The dealing-with-libertarians issue is settled.

The other major issue—whether Objectivism is open or closed—remains as the only major point of difference (though it has implications for the issues of toleration and error vs. evil, as I discussed in the book).

In Chapter 5, I reviewed two arguments for holding that Objectivism is a closed system of ideas, including all but only the philosophical views Ayn Rand put forth during her life. The first is that a philosophical system by nature is a totality of logically integrated principles that is *complete*, covering every major issue in philosophy, and has a *fixed identity* in which no element can be changed without collapsing the entire system. The second argument is that Objectivism is the name Rand chose for her philosophical ideas; the term was hers to define and restrict; it's her intellectual property, like *Atlas Shrugged*. I examined both these arguments at length, showing why they are not sound.

Along the way, I criticized Leonard Peikoff's view that Objectivism has an authorized doctrine. That view, I said,

> ... leaves us with two alternatives. We may treat consistency with [Rand's] writings as a value to be achieved at all costs, trimming our mental sails to ensure that result. Or we may remain loyal to our perception of the facts and be prepared to announce that we are not Objectivists, should we find ourselves in disagreement with even the least fundamental of her philosophical ideas. To be Objectivists, in other words, we must abandon rationality; to be rational, we must be ready at any moment to abandon Objectivism. (pp. 82–83 of this volume)

In a recent interview defending the closed position, Yaron Brook seemed to affirm the point: "Some of what Rand said might be wrong. It doesn't include every aspect of philosophy. Is Objectivism equal to the truth? No!" Instead, he relied mainly on the second argument that the name "Objectivism" was Rand's to define.[2]

As far as I can understand, Brook's comments reduce the open vs. closed dispute to a semantic issue about the referent of the term "Objectivism." Can that be all there is to 30 years of acrimony?

For my part, as an Objectivist philosopher who considers the essential principles Rand discovered to be true and who seeks further truths on that basis, I now find the closed view even more perplexing than I did 30 years ago. Among the many questions:

- If "Objectivism" is a name for the totality of Ayn Rand's philosophical beliefs—but nothing more, less, or different from them in any respect, how do we determine which of her statements are philosophical and which are not? For example, the central third of Galt's speech, as well as portions of Rand's other writings, are analyses of the motives for altruism, mysticism, collectivism, etc. Are these philosophical claims? Or are they psychological or historical claims? Can Objectivists disagree about which statements are philosophical and which are not?
- In Chapter 5, I outlined what I consider the essential tenets of Objectivism as a philosophy. What additional tenets would advocates of the closed view add? What additional tenets would

they require someone to hold before acknowledging the person as an Objectivist?

- Can anyone other than Rand call themselves an Objectivist? The meaning of the statements she made or endorsed depends on their conceptual content. How does one tell whether one has understood the content in her mind? Can Objectivists disagree about what Rand meant by a given philosophical statement?
- If Rand had not identified a major thesis of Objectivism, like self-esteem as a cardinal value, but someone else (e.g., Branden) had done so and even come up with the formulation "competent to live and worthy of life," would the thesis not be part of Objectivism?

A debate about these questions would be interesting and illuminating—as open discussion and debate are on other issues, in ethics, or epistemology, or whatever. Before I parted company with my former peers, I had countless conversations along these lines, as I do now with my colleagues. Even then, to be sure, we tried to be careful about what was a clearly worked-out element of Objectivism and what was speculation. But in scores of conversations with Peikoff and others, where we discussed new issues, and questioned some of Rand's ideas, I do not remember anyone raising the issue of whether Objectivism is open or closed.

In any case, there *have* been advances in Objectivist theory over the past 30 years. To mention a few of the more important ones:

- Nathaniel Branden expanded our understanding of self-esteem. In particular, his book *The Six Pillars of Self-Esteem* gave philosophical as well as psychological insight about this cardinal value of Objectivism.
- My case for benevolence as an Objectivist virtue, in *Unrugged Individualism: the Selfish Basis of Benevolence,* drew on Rand's novels as well as the internal logic of the Objectivist ethics to show why benevolence is a necessary means to our values.
- *The Logical Leap,* by David Harriman and Leonard Peikoff, presented the first systematic Objectivist treatment of induction, which Rand herself recognized as a gap in her epistemology.

I could mention many other insightful works. The thousands upon thousands of articles, books, courses, and intellectual journals created in the years since Rand died are not merely regurgitations of her words or ideas. When we winnow the wheat from the chaff, we are still left with a rich body of Objectivist thought from which we can expand the philosophy as an open, growing intellectual movement. While Rand was alive, thinkers inspired by her naturally sought her opinion on their work. What better teacher or reviewer could one have?

But she is gone. We're on our own. It's time to take responsibility for the philosophical wealth we inherited and, like Francisco d'Anconia, aim to multiply it.

Notes

I am indebted to Joan and Allan Blumenthal, Roger Donway, James Lennox, and George Walsh for valuable comments and criticism on earlier drafts of this essay. The responsibility for everything contained in the essay, however, is entirely my own; their generous help does not imply agreement with my views. To the many other people who have written me regarding this controversy, I would like to offer my heartfelt if anonymous thanks for their insight, advice, and moral support.

Introduction

1. Peter Schwartz, "On Sanctioning the Sanctioners," *Intellectual Activist* IV (Feb. 27, 1989).
2. Leonard Peikoff, "Fact and Value," *Intellectual Activist* V (May18, 1989). Cited hereafter as FV.
3. Ayn Rand, *Introduction to Objectivist Epistemology*, 2nd ed., ed. Harry Binswanger and Leonard Peikoff (New York: New American Library, 1979), chap. 8. See also David Kelley, *The Evidence of the Senses* (Baton Rouge: Louisiana State University Press, 1986), chap. 1.
4. Ayn Rand, "What is Capitalism?" in *Capitalism: The Unknown Ideal* (New York: Penguin Books, 1967), p. 22.

I. Moral Judgment

1. Ayn Rand, "The Objectivist Ethics," in *The Virtue of Selfishness* (New York: Penguin Books, 1964), pp. 13–39.
2. FV, p. 1, emphasis added. Peikoff cites Ayn Rand's statement ("The Objectivist Ethics," p. 24) that "'Knowledge, for any conscious organism, is the means of survival; to a living consciousness, every '*is*' implies an '*ought*'." Since this statement is not elaborated, and since it occurs in a passage that is not concerned with the issues Peikoff and I are debating, I am not sure that his interpretation of the statement is correct. Suffice it to say that if she meant what he takes her to mean, then I disagree with her, for the reasons adduced in the text.

3. In logic, a proposition of the form "All S are P" implies "Some P are S," not "All P are S." Inferring the latter proposition is a fallacy known as illicit conversion. See my *Art of Reasoning*, 4th ed. (New York: W. W. Norton, 2013), pp. 163–66.
4. Peikoff slides back and forth between fact, cognition, and truth—and between value, evaluation, and evil—in a manner that comes close to a formal equivocation. One especially slippery formulation is the claim that the good is a species of the true, the evil a species of the false (FV, p. 1). Sunlight is good for us, tidal waves bad, but neither of them is either true or false; they are facts of reality, not assertions by a consciousness.
5. I would also say that the concept of "evil" is restricted to the moral realm. Though the term is sometimes used to describe anything that causes harm or suffering, it normally implies a wicked motive.
6. This statement should not be taken to mean that the choice to think or not is the fundamental choice in the Objectivist moral code as such. In particular, I do not hold that it is more fundamental than the choice to live. The relationship between these two choices is complex, but it is not at issue here.
7. See Kelley, *The Evidence of the Senses,* chaps. 1, 3.
8. Cf. Robert James Bidinotto, "Facts, Values and Moral Sanctions: An Open letter to Objectivists" (www.vix.com/objectivism/Writing/RobertBidinotto/FactsValuesMoralSanctions.html), pp.12–14.
9. Cf. Ayn Rand, "The Cult of Moral Grayness," in *The Virtue of Selfishness,* p. 89: "Unless one is prepared to dispense with morality altogether and to regard a petty chiseller and a murderer as morally equal, one still has to judge and evaluate the many shadings of 'gray' that one may encounter in the characters of individual men."
10. Rand, Introduction to Objectivism Epistemology, pp. 42–43.
11. FV, p. 2.
12. Leonard Peikoff, "Why Should One Act on Principle?" *Intellectual Activist* IV, Feb. 27, 1989), p. 56.
13. FV, p. 5.

14. Cf. Ayn Rand, "How Does One Lead a Rational Life in an Irrational Society?" in *The Virtue of Selfishness,* p. 84: "To judge means: to evaluate a given concrete by reference to an abstract principle or standard. It is not an easy task; it is not a task that can be performed automatically by one's feelings, 'instinct,' or hunches. It is a task that requires the most precise, the most exacting, the most ruthlessly objective and *rational* process of thought. It is fairly easy to grasp abstract moral principles; it can be very difficult to apply them to a given situation, particularly when it involves the moral character of another person." Given this emphatic statement about the requirements of moral judgment, I have reservations about her assertion elsewhere in the essay (p. 84) that "one must know clearly, in full, verbally identified form, one's own moral evaluation of every person, issue and event with which one deals...." Unless she intended this to be subject to the qualifications I have discussed, I think it is an overstatement. It would certainly be valuable to have the knowledge she describes, but I see no basis in the Objectivist ethics for holding that we must pursue this value at the cost of all others.
15. This point is developed much further in my book *Unrugged Individualism: The Selfish Basis of Benevolence* (Poughkeepsie, NY: The Objectivist Center, 1996), chap. 7. There I discussed how productiveness in the material realm and benevolence in the social realm are virtues concerned with creating value—i.e., bringing something new into existence—by contrast, respectively, with rationality and justice, which are concerned with identifying and evaluating what already exists.

II. Sanction

1. In the previous chapter, I noted that the term "evil" is normally restricted to the moral realm (see note 5). Traditionally the term was used as the most general antithesis of good, referring to natural conditions such as sickness, and natural disasters such as floods, as well as to human vice, corruption, malice, etc. Today, that broad function of the term has largely been superseded by the word "bad"; "evil" is more commonly

restricted now to things that can be evaluated as morally bad. Within the moral realm, moreover, the term is usually (but not always) reserved for wrongdoing or vice of the highest degree, as measured both by consequences and by motives. When Rand uses the term in formulating her principle regarding the impotence of evil, and when Peikoff uses it in our debate about error vs. evil (the topic of Chapter 3), I believe they intend to equate evil with wrongdoing as such, with anything that is morally culpable, rather than limiting it to a high degree of wrongdoing. For the sake of this discussion, I have followed the same usage in this and succeeding chapters.

2. I would no longer say that issues of sanction arise only in cases where moral culpability is involved. One may oppose and take action to withhold aid from a people or groups that one believes are acting contrary to one's values even if one believes they are innocently mistaken in their beliefs and pursuits.
3. Peter Schwartz, "On Moral Sanctions," *Intellectual Activist* V (May 18, 1989), p. 7.
4. Ayn Rand, "The Anatomy of Compromise," in *Capitalism: The Unknown Ideal,* p. 145.
5. Several people have drawn my attention to the fact that Ayn Rand dealt with precisely this point in connection with a charge by Senate liberals that Justice William Rehnqulst once spoke to a right-wing group: "This is an insidious kind of intimidation: it equates a speaker's views with those of the discussion's sponsors. A man of integrity is conscientiously precise about the nature of his views on any subject. If his views are going to be judged, not by his own statements, but by the views of those who invite him to speak... then his only alternative is to accept no speaking engagements. If so, what happens to our freedom of speech?" "The Disenfranchisement of the Right," *The Ayn Rand Letter* I (Dec.20, 1971), p. 26.
6. Rand, "Anatomy of Compromise," p. 145.
7. This summary of Schwartz's view is drawn not only from "On Moral Sanctions" but also from an earlier essay, "Libertarianism: The Perversion of Liberty," *Intellectual Activist* III–IV (May 10, 1985–Dec. 4, 1985); reprinted in Ayn Rand, *The Voice of*

Reason: Essays in Objectivist Thought, ed. Leonard Peikoff (New York: Penguin Books, 1989), pp. 311–333.

8. Schwartz, "On Moral Sanctions," p. 7.
9. Ibid.

III. Error and Evil

1. This is the basic pattern of all teleological assessment, as Aristotle observed. The evaluation of the end or outcome is logically prior to the evaluation of the means or cause.
2. This was the point I was trying to make in "A Question of Sanction" when I said: "Soviet tyrants are not evil because they believe in Marxian collectivism. They are evil because they have murdered millions of people and enslaved hundreds of millions more."
3. FV, pp. 2–3.
4. FV, pp. 3–4, emphasis added.
5. The discussion in the text is concerned with Peikoff's claim that Kant's ideas were causally sufficient for the disasters of the 20th century. But he also asserts that the ideas are necessary conditions: "Without the philosophical climate Kant and his intellectual followers created, none of these disasters could have occurred." This is an extraordinary claim: that no other set of conditions could have led to totalitarianism. How would one support this negative claim? And how can it be squared with the oppression, war, and bloodshed that have occurred throughout mankind's history without benefit of Kant? During the French Revolution, to pick only one example, the Reign of Terror under Robespierre exhibited most of the features of Soviet and Nazi totalitarianism: the political use of terror, secret informers, the demonization of a class blamed for social problems, prosecution of economic crimes, show trials, etc. To the extent that this episode was inspired by philosophical ideas, they were the ideas of Rousseau, not Kant.
6. Leonard Peikoff, "Philosophy and Psychology in History," *Objectivist Forum* 6 (Oct. 1985), pp. 10, 14.
7. FV, p. 2.

8. Ayn Rand, "This is John Galt Speaking," in *For the New Intellectual* (New York: Penguin Books, 1961), p. 136.
9. FV, p. 4.
10. The extreme form of the fallacy described in this paragraph is a crude sort of conspiracy theory to the effect that an ideology like Marxism, which had awful consequences, is a smokescreen put out in order to disguise the deliberate pursuit of those consequences. An example is Schwartz's statement in "On Moral Sanctions," p. 6 that "the theory of Marxism gains acceptance by declaring that it seeks to eradicate unfair exploitation, not that it desires to impose totalitarian enslavement."
11. Ayn Rand, "Faith and Force: The Destroyers of the Modern World," in *Philosophy: Who Needs It* (New York: Penguin Books, 1982), p. 61.
12. Peikoff claims that I offered the academic Marxist as an example of innocent error (FV, p. 3). Soviet Russia. I was speaking of consequences, not motives. I said the Marxist was guilty of an intellectual error; I did not say or imply anything about whether the error was honest. (In fact, I believe that few Marxists are innocently mistaken.) Indeed, in the very next paragraph of "A Question of Sanction," I said that one cannot tell solely from the content of a man's belief whether its source is rational or not. Of all the misrepresentations in Peikoff's essay, this is one of the clearest and most irresponsible.
13. FV, p. 3.
14. FV, pp. 2–3.
15. See, for example, Peikoff's lecture course, "Understanding Objectivism," lecture 10.
16. FV, p. 5.
17. Cognitive psychologists have done extensive research on thinking errors that are committed through apparent ignorance of relevant standards. Kenneth Livingston has used the Objectivist theory of concepts to propose an explanation for such errors. Kenneth R. Livingston, Rationality and the Psychology of Abstraction (Poughkeepsie, NY: The Objectivist Center, 1998).
18. FV, p. 3.
19. FV, p. 4.

20. The foregoing discussion presented the reasons why a person's acceptance of a false idea may or may not involve irrationality on his part. I would also argue, on similar grounds, that a person's acceptance of a true idea may or may not involve rationality. It is possible to accept a truth on the basis of authority, for example, rather than because one has a first-hand grasp of the evidence for its truth. One may even understand the structure of reasons for a doctrine but embrace the doctrine not because of the evidence per se but because it allows one to be an iconoclast, or because the doctrine rationalizes a hostile desire to denounce other people—to mention a few nonrational motives for belief.
21. Rand, "This is John Galt Speaking," p. 149.
22. Rand, *For the New Intellectual,* pp. 15, 16.
23. Kelley, *The Evidence Of the Senses,* chap. 1.

IV. Tolerance

1. FV, p. 5.
2. Rand, *Introduction to Objectivist Epistemology,* chap. 7.
3. John Stuart Mill, *On Liberty,* ed. David Spitz (New York: W. W. Norton, 1975), p. 36.
4. Ibid., p. 21.
5. This statement is ambiguous at best because of a careless use of the term "context." Epistemologically, the term refers to the body of observations, concepts, logical relationships, and prior conclusions that are relevant to a given conclusion. In other words, the context of a given conclusion consists of cognitive contents within the mind of the individual drawing the conclusion. By the very nature of mental contents, this context is a possession of the individual; it is not social or collective in any sense. Context in this sense is quite distinct from the social context of other thinkers with whom one can profitably engage in discussion and debate.

V. Objectivism

1. FV, pp. 5–6.
2. Ibid.

3. Rand, *For the New Intellectual,* p. 14ff.
4. I include in this assessment the whole of her *Introduction to Objectivist Epistemology*; the whole of *For the New Intellectual,* which includes all the philosophical passages from her novels; all of her theoretical essays in ethics, politics, and aesthetics; and her essays about the nature of philosophy and particular philosophers. The total comes to something under 600 pages, about the length of a standard college reader that brings together the important writings of a philosopher.
5. An authorized doctrine, of course, requires an authority to say what it is. An interview with Peikoff in the Ayn Rand Institute's *Newsletter* 8.1 (Feb. 1993), contained this remarkable passage:

   > Q. What do you like and dislike about being the spokesman of Objectivism?
   > A. I like having the power to make definitive statements on philosophic ques- tions. I'm in a position to judge whether a particular view is essential to Objectivism, a betrayal of it, or purely optional—and then to make my own view emphatically known.... I like being the guardian of the philosophy's integrity....

   As Peikoff himself would be the first to acknowledge, however, the logic of his position implies that Ayn Rand is the only real authority, and she is no longer alive to say which statements and works by other thinkers she considers consistent with her own views. As a result, orthodox scholars have engaged in tortured attempts to explain whether and in exactly what way their own works are to be seen as expressions of Objectivism. Once again, as the intellectual leader, Peikoff provides the best example, in his *Objectivism: The Philosophy of Ayn Rand* (New York: Dutton, 1991), p. xv:

   > Because of my thirty years of study under her, and by her own statement, I am the person next to Ayn Rand who is the most qualified to write this book. Since she did not live to see it, however, she is not responsible for any misstatements of her views it may contain, nor can the book be

> properly described as 'official Objectivist doctrine.' 'Objectivism' is the name of Ayn Rand's philosophy as presented in the material she herself wrote or endorsed.
> To be objective, I identify the status of my work as follows: this book is the definitive statement of Ayn Rand's philosophy—as interpreted by her best student and chosen heir.

The tortured quality of this passage lies partly in Peikoff's attempt to define a derivative mode of authority he can claim for himself. If, as he claims, he is the best interpreter of her thought ("her best student"), it is a status he has earned by the merit of his work as a writer and teacher. But he goes on fallaciously to cite Rand's authority (he is "her chosen heir") as an additional basis for his status. Rand's own view about who best understands the principles she discovered certainly deserves respect, but in the end this is an issue of who actually excels by the objective standards of scholarship, an issue to be settled by the facts, not by anyone's opinion.

The passage is also a tortured effort to comply with Peikoff's view that Objectivism has an official doctrine He acknowledges that his own formulations cannot be described as official Objectivist doctrine because they do not consist of Rand's own words or words she approved. Presumably the reader himself must judge whether and to what extent Peikoff's work is consistent with Rand's. This means that even if one accepts the notion of an official Objectivist doctrine, the question of what is and is not consistent with it must be established by proof, not authority. It also makes one wonder what the point of having an official doctrine is supposed to be. Is acceptance of the official doctrine supposed to be a means of grasping reality? That would be an obviously fallacious appeal to authority, a case of epistemological second-handedness. And it would be futile in any case. We have to exercise independent thought and apply the canons of objective proof in order to identify what is consistent with Rand's words, so why not apply these cognitive tools to identify the facts of reality directly—as Ayn Rand herself had to do? Or is the acceptance of official doctrine supposed to serve merely as a criterion of who counts as an Objectivist? Here again, we would have to use our own judgment to determine whether a given's thinker's philosophical views are consistent with Rand's words. But the more important problem is the definition of "Objectivism" in this fashion to begin with—for all the reasons outlined in the text. As a philosophical school of thought, it cannot be defined by an official doctrine to begin with.

6. FV, p. 5.
7. Ibid.
8. These observations about the inductive basis of philosophical principles and the non-obvious character of the logical connections among those principles are explained in much more detail in William R Thomas and David Kelley, *The Logical Structure of Objectivism* (Poughkeepsie, NY: The Objectivist Center, forthcoming).
9. Ibid.
10. Ayn Rand, "Patents and Copyrights," in *Capitalism: The Unknown Ideal*, pp. 130–134.
11. Ayn Rand's own view on the name "Objectivism" was stated in four essays: "A Message to Our Readers," by Nathaniel Branden, *Objectivist Newsletter* 4 (Apr. 1965); "A Letter from a Reader," by Ayn Rand, Objectivist 5 (Oct. 1966); "A Statement of Policy," by Ayn Rand and Henry Holzer, *Objectivist* 7 (June-July 1968); and "To the Readers of the Objectivist Forum," by Ayn Rand, *Objectivist Forum* 1 (Feb. 1980). The essential points in these articles, as best I can interpret them, are the following:

    i. Rand wanted to protect the integrity of her system of ideas from people who got it wrong or who distorted its meaning by embracing only part of it. This is an understandable goal, and indeed a responsibility of an original thinker.
    ii. She claimed the right to determine who could put his views forth under the name Objectivism and which writings were considered expressions of Objectivism. This point goes beyond (i) in its assertion of control. Rand acknowledged that she had no such *legal* right, that she did not own the term "Objectivism" as she did the titles and characters of the

novels, or her own name. She claimed a *moral* right to control the term, however, because she had created its public value. But just as the cognitive content of an idea cannot be owned except insofar as it is embodied in a specific product, so the value of an idea's public reputation cannot be owned except insofar as it is embodied in a particular expression such as a title. Rand deserves respect, gratitude, and public credit for popularizing the Objectivist philosophy no less than for discovering its principles. But that entitlement does not extend to control over the independent judgment of other thinkers in determining what is and is not consistent with those principles.

iii. In these same articles, and elsewhere, Rand made it clear that she wanted Objectivism as a philosophy to spread among intellectuals and the culture at large, and that she knew its spread would be the work of independent thinkers. For the reasons mentioned in the text, the moral "right" she claimed is not consistent with this goal.

12. Ayn Rand, "Introducing Objectivism," *Objectivist Newsletter* 1 (Aug. 1962): 35.
13. Richard B. Salsman criticized this passage in "From the AOB Mailbag: 'Pseudo-Tolerationism,'" *AOB News* (newsletter of the Association of Objectivist Businessmen), Spring 1994. "Honesty is not merely some 'point' in Objectivism, as [Kelley] says but a central virtue, derived painstakingly from the cardinal virtue of rationality (which he concedes) and from the very nature of reality." In accordance with the Objectivist theory of defining concepts by essentials, however, the fact that the virtue of honesty is derived from the virtue of rationality makes the latter the more essential feature of the Objectivist ethics. And the fact that the derivation needs to be "painstaking" is a reflection of the many issues involved, about which Objectivist thinkers can reasonably disagree.
14. FV, p. 5.
15. Ibid.
16. Ayn Rand, "The Missing Link," in *Philosophy: Who Needs It*, pp. 38, 41.

17. An amusing if pathetic example of this attitude is the following statement from a newsletter of a local Objectivist club, commenting on the question of what the term "Objectivism" means:

    > To use the name Objectivism for a philosophy with which Ayn Rand would have disagreed is thievery.... Imagine you are a youngster who is known by neighborhood kids as a friend of—and sometimes spokesman for—the base- ball coach. The baseball coach has led his team with 'Coach's Ten Rules for Winning Ball Games.' Now Coach leaves town and you step in to guide the team. It would be wrong for you to change Rule #6 and still call the list 'Coach's Ten Rules,' knowing that Coach would not approve the change. A kid in a playground can understand this. And a layman can understand that professing to teach Ayn Rand's philosophy while changing it is wrong. [Bay Area Students of Objectivism Newsletter, April 1991, John P. McCaskey, editor]

    If I were trying to write a satire or parody of true-believing Objectivists, I could not have done better than this. The notion that Objectivism is comparable to a set of ten rules, like the Ten Commandments, is the perfect expression of the concrete-bound approach described in the text.
18. FV, pp. 5–6.
19. As with these other intellectual tribes, orthodox Objectivists reserve their fiercest hatred for "apostates"—Objectivists who do not participate in the orthodox movement because of disagreements with its leaders. The Ayn Rand Institute has made it clear to the campus clubs it sponsors that all support will be withdrawn if a club invites me as a speaker—or anyone from The Objectivist Center or anyone associated with us—even with the club's own money. Lyceum, an Objectivist conference organization, refused to send a conference brochure to someone who had lectured at our Summer Seminar. "Our policy," said the head of the organization, "is to remove anyone from our mailing list who is speaking at any [Institute for Objectivist Studies] functions" [Private letter]. The Objectivist Society of

Los Angeles asserted, in its 1996 "Statement of Principles," that support for either the Libertarian Party or "the Institute for Objectivist Studies directed by David Kelley" is incompatible with Objectivism; applicants for membership must sign the following oath: "I have read and understood the OSLA Statement of Principles, and agree to abide by its policies. I certify that I am not a supporter of the Libertarian Party or The Institute for Objectivist Studies."

This is the most puzzling aspect of the tribal attitude to many people, who can't understand why thinkers sharing the same philosophy should be such bitter enemies. But it is in fact the logical extension of the attitude I have analyzed in the text, and it is a common historical pattern. The early Christian church never went after infidels and pagans with the same ferocity it exercised toward Jews, and even more toward heretics within Christianity. The Freudian psychoanalysts never attacked behaviorism, their polar opposite in the field of psychology, with the same venom they expressed toward innovators in their own movement like Carl Jung.

The reason for this pattern is that apostates, heretics, innovators do not simply challenge some of the movement's ideas. If that were all, then it would indeed be incomprehensible why orthodox adherents of a creed are much more bothered by these relatively small areas of disagreement than with the wholesale differences from their philosophical or ideological opponents. But innovators also challenge—they reject—the authority of the movement's leaders. This is an issue of method that goes far beyond the substance of any new idea or reform that the innovator puts forward. In substantive terms, he may have called into question only a small portion of the movement's system of belief. But he has *completely* rejected the *method* by which true believers embrace that system. Nothing could be more threatening. The apostate also threatens the true believer by his willingness to risk exclusion from the movement, putting his own ideas and his own judgment ahead of membership in the group. To those for whom membership is essential to their very sense of identity, again, nothing could be more threatening—especially if the doctrine they profess is one that regards independence as a virtue.

20. Barbara Branden, *The Passion of Ayn Rand* (Garden City, NY: Doubleday, 1986).
21. Peter Schwartz, letter to readers of *Intellectual Activist*, Aug. 20, 1986.
22. Leonard Peikoff, "My Thirty Years with Ayn Rand: An Intellectual Memoir," in *Objectivist Forum* 8 (1987), p. 15; reprinted in *Ayn Rand: The Voice of Reason* (New York: Penguin Books, 1990), p. 352.
23. Rand, "The Missing Link," p. 54.

Postscript

1. "[W]e see evidence to suggest that there is no longer a cohesive libertarian movement. The movement has become fragmented and leaderless (intellectually as well as organizationally)....

   "The term 'libertarian' has been used increasingly over the last few years to mean a vague leaning toward liberty rather than government control....

   "However, none of the three political terms — 'liberal,' 'conservative,' or 'libertarian' — has a clearly defined meaning, because there exist no clearly defined ideologies." ["What is ARI's view of the libertarian movement?" https://ari.aynrand.org/faq (accessed January 10, 2019).] Most libertarian theorists and organizations would find these claims surprising, to say the least.
2. "Ayn Rand made the simple request that Objectivism be the name given to all the ideas as they are expressed in her books and her lectures and the things that she authorized." Yaron Brook, video interview by Tomasz Kołodziejczuk at FreedomFest 2016, "Why Closed Objectivism?" https://www.youtube.com/watch?v=WyNgRhQls1o (accessed January 10, 2019).

Appendix A: A Question of Sanction

An Open Letter, March, 1989

> [This open letter was written in response to an article Peter Schwartz published in *The Intellectual Activist* in early 1989. I sent copies to about 30 people, including Schwartz himself and Leonard Peikoff, and authorized anyone to copy and distribute it further. Within a few weeks it had circulated widely in the Objectivist movement. Peikoff's "Fact and Value" was written in response to it.]

A number of people have asked me about "On Sanctioning the Sanctioners" (*The Intellectual Activist 2/27/89*), which was in part an attack on me for speaking to libertarian groups. In response, I want to set the record straight regarding my own actions, and to identify certain attitudes in the article that I think are incompatible with a philosophy of reason.

In addition to my philosophical work over the last fifteen years, I have been a polemicist for freedom. In scores of articles and speeches, my goal has been to defend individual rights on an Objectivist foundation— as clearly and forcefully as I can to as wide an audience as possible. As a polemicist, my efforts are naturally directed at people who are not already Objectivists. To reach that audience I must speak to groups and write for publications that do not share my ideas. In using these channels of communication, I try to make sure that my association with them does not put me in the position of endorsing ideas I reject. That would defeat my purpose. But I cannot engage my opponents without conferring some benefit on them, in some indirect and attenuated fashion—buying their books, helping them retain their audience, or the like. If every such benefit is to be condemned as aiding the enemy, then one cannot participate in the marketplace of ideas. One can only preach to the converted—a sorry sort of ingrown activism.

In any given case, therefore, I weigh the costs of association against the possible gains. Before I accept a writing or speaking engagement, I consider whether my sponsors are offering me access to an audience I could not otherwise have reached; or whether I would be helping them attract an audience *they* could not otherwise have earned. I consider whether my sponsors have a definite editorial policy or ideological commitment opposed to Objectivism, and, if so, whether they are willing to have me state my disagreement explicitly. I consider whether the format of my appearance would suggest that I endorse other speakers and their views. And I consider what I know of their moral and intellectual character. In weighing these and other matters, I am always looking for long-range strategic gain at minimal cost. That's how you fight a war of ideas.

In the case of libertarians, I have turned down many invitations because I felt the costs outweighed any likely gain. But the balance sometimes tips the other way. I recently spoke at the Laissez Faire Supper Club on the role of Objectivism in defending freedom—the incident to which Peter Schwartz refers in his articles. I have also accepted an invitation to speak on the ethical foundations of rights at the Cato Institute's Summer Seminar in July. Of the factors that affected these decisions, the following are the most important:

- Libertarianism is a broadly defined movement. The subjectivists represent one definite wing of the movement, and we cannot make common cause with them. But they are not the only or even the predominant wing. Many who describe themselves as libertarians recognize that rights must be grounded in a rational, secular, and individualist moral philosophy. I know and have worked with many such people, and I regard them as potential allies in the cause of liberty. I have generally found them open to Objectivist ideas, so long as one doesn't harangue them in a spirit of sectarian hostility. When I was invited to speak at the Cato seminar, for example, the organizers were enthusiastic about my proposal to explain why Ayn Rand's ethics is a better foundation for rights than any alternative.
- Laissez Faire Books is not a magazine with an editorial policy, or a party with a platform. It is a book service, selling works that take many different positions on philosophical issues. Unlike a general-

purpose book store, it deals primarily with works that are relevant to a free market, but within that range the owners select books primarily on the basis of what will interest their customers. This includes virtually anything on Objectivism, pro or con. One can certainly quarrel with some of their selections, but one cannot accuse them of loading the dice against us. They are eager to sell Ayn Rand's own works, as well as the contributions her followers have made to the literature. I am delighted that they have brought our work to the attention of their customers, some of whom were not previously familiar with Objectivism, and I have autographed copies of *The Evidence of the Senses* as a way to help sales. In doing so, I was not endorsing or supporting any work but my own. Nor do I "promote" the bookstore, as Schwartz claims, except in the sense of regarding it as a legitimate commercial enterprise.

- The same principle applies to the Supper Club they sponsor. In appearing there, I was not, as Schwartz says, an after-dinner speaker at a libertarian function. I *was* the function. The sole purpose of the occasion was to hear my explanation of why individual rights and capitalism cannot be established without reference to certain key principles of Objectivism: the absolutism of reason, the rejection of altruism, and the commitment to life in this world as a primary value. Since I explicitly criticized libertarian ideas that are incompatible with those principles, I was obviously not endorsing them.

Such, in brief, is the reasoning that has governed my conduct as a public advocate of Objectivism. Peter Schwartz regards it as transparently wrong, beyond any possibility of honest disagreement. He asserts that libertarians are the moral "equivalent" of the Soviet regime, and I the equivalent of Armand Hammer. These are wild accusations, preposterous on their face. But they exhibit a kind of zealotry that has a wider significance than the fact that Second Renaissance doesn't carry my works. I want to comment on three specific issues.

1) A sense of proportion. Even if we accepted the premise that libertarianism as such is a vice, there would be a vast difference of degree between libertarians and a regime that has the blood of millions on its hands. When we formulate moral principles, we may abstract from such differences of degree; we omit measurements, as Ayn Rand explained. But when we *apply* the principles in forming moral judgments about particulars, we must reintroduce the relevant measurements. Just as one diminishes the good by praising mediocrity, one trivializes evil by damning the venial. If libertarians are no better than Soviet dictators, then Soviet dictators are no worse than libertarians. Those who indulge in moral hysteria—condemning all moral error with the same fury, without regard to differences of degree—destroy their own credibility when it comes to the depths of evil: the Stalins, the Hitlers, the Ayatollah.

2) Evil vs. error. A cardinal principle of Objectivist ethics is that one should not give evil the moral sanction it needs to justify itself and disarm its victims. And a principle of responsible advocacy is that one should not endorse false ideas. These principles are related but they are not the same, because evil and error are not the same.

The concept of evil applies primarily to actions, and to the people who perform them. Schwartz asserts that we should not sanction the Soviets because they are "philosophical enemies." This is a bizarre interpretation of their sins. Soviet tyrants are not evil because they believe in Marxian collectivism. They are evil because they have murdered millions of people and enslaved hundreds of millions more. An academic Marxist who subscribes to the same ideas as Lenin or Stalin does not have the same moral status. He is guilty of the same intellectual error, but not of their crimes (unless and to the extent that he actively supported them, as many did in the 1930s, although even here we must recognize a difference in degree of culpability).

Truth and falsity, not good or evil, are the primary evaluative concepts that apply to ideas as such. It is true that the horrors of this century were made possible by irrationalist and collectivist ideas. Bad ideas can be dangerous; that's one reason we shouldn't endorse them. But they are dangerous because *people* use them to perpetrate evil. We are not Hegelians: ideas per se are not agents in the world. Truth or falsity is the essential property of an idea; the good or ill it produces is derivative. It is also true that a given person may adopt false ideas through evasion, which is morally wrong. But another person might adopt the same idea through honest error. The assumption that libertarians as such are immoral is therefore an egregious insult. Some are honest and rational, some are not. The same is true for any other ideological group, including Objectivists. It is a gross *non-sequitur* to infer that because an idea is false, its adherents are evil for holding it.

The failure to draw these distinctions has a pernicious effect. If we approach ideas with the question: true or false?, we stand ready to combat bad ideas by the only means appropriate to intellectual issues: open, rational discussion and debate. But if we approach ideas with the question: good or evil?, we will avoid debate for fear of sanctioning evildoers. We will substitute condemnation for argument, and adopt a non-intellectual, intolerant attitude toward any disagreement with our views.

3) Tolerance. Tolerance is not a virtue where evil is concerned; evil flourishes by the tolerance of good people. But it *is* a virtue in the cognitive realm. It is appropriate not only among people who disagree about the application of principles they share, but also among people who disagree on the principles themselves. Tolerance is not a weak-kneed confession of uncertainty. It is a recognition that certainty is contextual. It is a recognition of the fact that knowledge is neither revealed nor invented, but acquired by an active process of integration; that any conclusion we reach is tied to reality by a long chain of reasoning, and presupposes an enormous context; and that open discussion and debate are the proper means of intellectual exchange.

To have any hope of persuading others, we must take the trouble to understand their context; we must approach them on an equal footing, a mutual willingness to be persuaded by the facts; and we must grant them time to sort through the issues and make sure that any new conclusion is rooted in their own grasp of reality. If we find that the other person is not open to reason, we should abandon the effort. Tolerance does not require that we beat our heads against the wall, or put up with willful irrationality. But we should assume that people *are* rational until we have evidence to the contrary. In this respect, tolerance is the intellectual expression of benevolence.

Benevolence has another and to my mind more important benefit: the growth of our own knowledge. There is much we can learn from others if we are willing to listen. And even where they are wrong, we strengthen the foundations of our own beliefs—the accuracy and range of our observations, the validity of our concepts, the rigor of our arguments—by the effort to prove *why* they are wrong.

That's why every age of reason has welcomed diversity and debate. The great minds of the Enlightenment declared war on the entire apparatus of intolerance: the obsession with official or authorized doctrine, the concepts of heresy and blasphemy, the party lines and intellectual xenophobia, the militant hostility among rival sects, the constant schisms and breaks, the character assassination of those who fall from grace. These are the techniques of irrational philosophies, such as Christianity or Marxism, and may well have been vital to their success. But they have no place in a philosophy of reason.

Ayn Rand left us a magnificent system of ideas. But it is not a closed system. It is a powerful engine of integration. Let us not starve it of fuel by shutting our minds to what is good in other approaches. Let us test our ideas in open debate. If we are right, we have nothing to fear; if we are wrong, we have something to learn. Above all, let us encourage independent thought among ourselves. Let us welcome dissent, and the restless ways of the explorers among us. Nine out of ten new ideas will be mistakes, but the tenth will let in the light.

David Kelley

Appendix B: A Note about Open Objectivism

October 2008

They say that fish can't see the water they swim in. It's a common analogy for the tendency to take our basic values and principles so much for granted that they become invisible. But to stay on track, we sometimes need to make those values and principles conscious, to remind ourselves where we are going, and why.

From the very beginning, the basic goal of The Atlas Society as an organization has been our mission of promoting Objectivism. Our basic principle—what has always defined and distinguished us—is the conviction that Objectivism is an open philosophy. That conviction is so deeply rooted in the way we function that we have long taken it for granted. In the course of reviewing our current programs and long-term strategy, however, we gained a new appreciation of how crucially important this principle is, especially in these troubled times, to the mission in which we and you, our partners and supporters, are engaged.

I'd like to share with you, our contributing members, our vision of open Objectivism. In essence, it means three things:

1) A commitment to reasoned, non-dogmatic discussion and debate.

People need to think for themselves, to reach conclusions they grasp first-hand through their own individual process of thought. That's true by the very nature of objective knowledge, and it's the reason why rationality and independence are moral virtues.

There's a natural tendency for movements and organizations to try to short-circuit the process by appealing to the authority of leaders or demanding total agreement. But that's not right. We know it's not right because it contradicts the Objectivist philosophy. But the Objectivist movement has sometimes succumbed to the tendency, with harmful results. If your experience is anything like mine, you have probably met people who might sympathize with our ideas but still keep their distance under the impression that Objectivism is some kind of sect.

That's one reason we feel it is still important to highlight our basic principle. The more important reason is the positive benefit we gain by respecting the rationality and independence of those we deal with. That policy starts with you, our members: we have always tried to earn your support by offering value rather than by guilt or intimidation. The policy applies to our events: those who have attended the Summer Seminar and other conferences have often said how empowering they found the spirit of open discussion and debate.

2) The recognition that Objectivism is open to expansion, refinement, and revision

Objectivism is a body of rational knowledge rather than a fixed, closed set of doctrines like a religion. This fact is implied by the very nature of human knowledge, which Objectivism teaches us is contextual, fallible, and open-ended. The philosophy itself must therefore be open to expansion, refinement, and, if necessary, revision in the same way as any other body of knowledge, such as Newtonian physics, the theory of evolution, market economics, etc.

To say that Objectivism is an open system is to invite discussion and debate, to welcome insights that can be verified and integrated, to recognize that the system can be revised if further inquiry reveals problems, and to acknowledge that there can be reasonable differences among honest Objectivists over specific issues. These are normal, healthy aspects of rational thought and cooperation among thinkers. They are based on respect for the independence of the individual, and they reflect the basic truth that the measure of a thinker is not agreement with a doctrine or a person, but agreement with the facts. In the long run, it is only by promulgating our philosophy in that spirit that we can achieve intellectual progress and attract people to the philosophy.

We have tried to practice these policies from the beginning. And, again, with tangible benefits, from the trust we have earned from our friends in academia, in other think tanks, and in the media; to the scholarly work we have sponsored and published ourselves; to the many innovative ideas you can find on our website.

3) A policy of benevolence toward others, including fellow-travelers and critics

One of those innovative ideas is that benevolence is a major virtue in Objectivism, and we now think of it as another dimension of openness. As I argued in *Unrugged Individualism: The Selfish Basis of Benevolence*, the essence of benevolence is not altruism. It is the virtue of seeking opportunities for trade by treating others with the basic respect they deserve as potential sources of value.

In the realm of ideas, benevolence means seeking opportunities for insight and knowledge, not only from other Objectivists, but also from opponents who raise intelligent questions and objections. And it means collaborating with other organizations where appropriate, in pursuit of common goals. As a minority position in the marketplace of ideas, we can expect to have an impact only if we take the initiative to engage with other positions—to make our case with passion, yes, but also to listen and learn, and to seek out willing allies in our cause.

And in that spirit, we welcome your thoughts, and we thank you for making our work possible.

David Kelley

Index

About the Author

David Kelley is an internationally respected philosopher, author, journalist, and lecturer. He is one of the world's foremost proponents of Ayn Rand's philosophy of Objectivism.

Dr. Kelley received his Ph. D. from Princeton University, and later taught philosophy at Vassar College and Brandeis University. In 1990 he founded The Atlas Society, a leading institute for research and education on Objectivism.

Dr. Kelley's books include *The Evidence of the Senses*, a treatise on the epistemology of sense-perception; *The Art of Reasoning*, a popular logic textbook; *A Life of One's Own: Individual Rights and the Welfare State*; and *Unrugged Individualism: The Selfish Basis of Benevolence*. He is also co-author of *The Logical Structure of Objectivism*. A former editorial writer for *Barron's*, he has also written for *Harper's*, *Reason*, *The Harvard Business Review* and other publications on a wide range of political and cultural issues. His guest appearances on the ABC News special, "'Greed' With John Stossel," stirred a national debate on the ethics of capitalism.

Made in the USA
San Bernardino, CA
20 February 2020